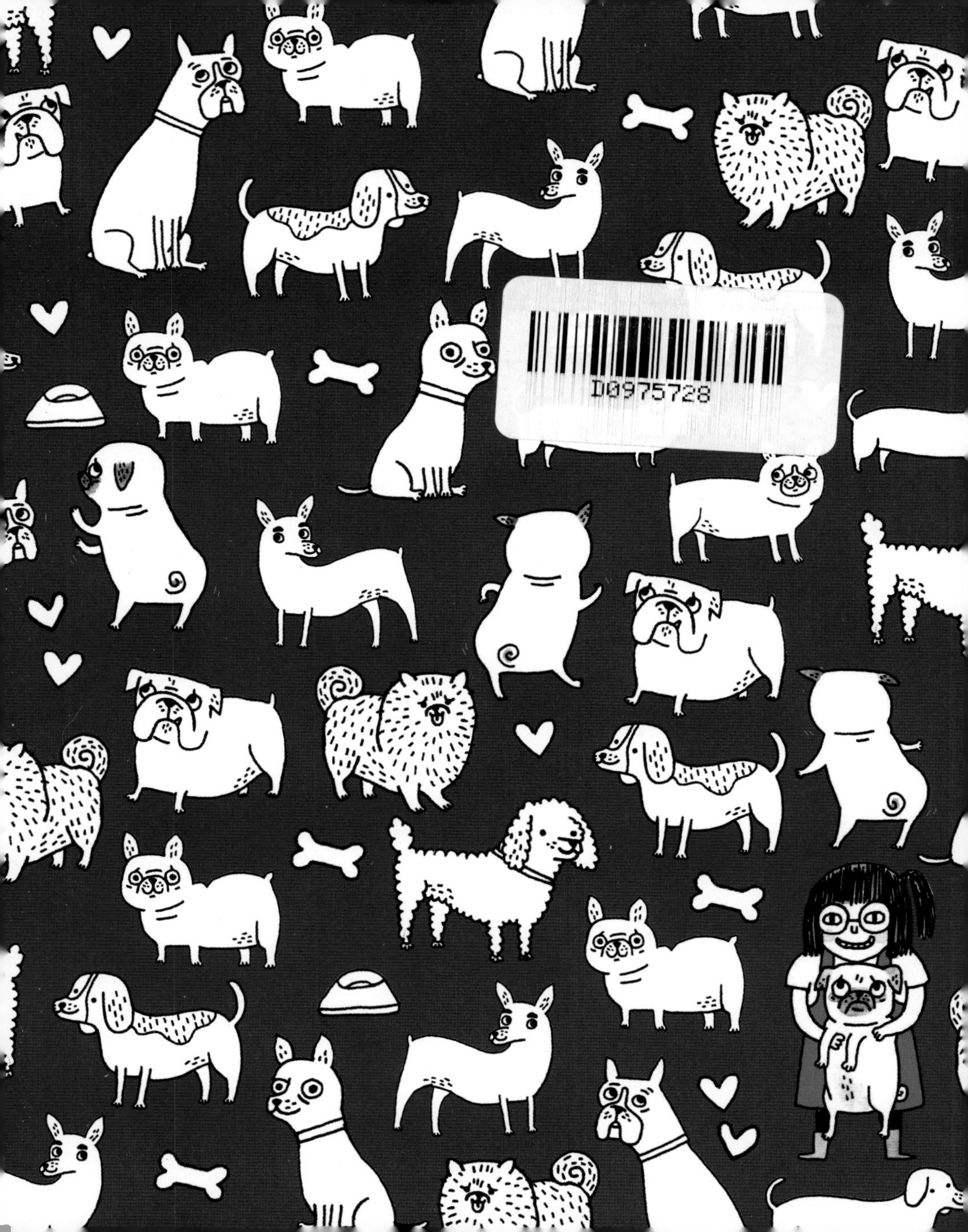

# A DOG'S LIFE

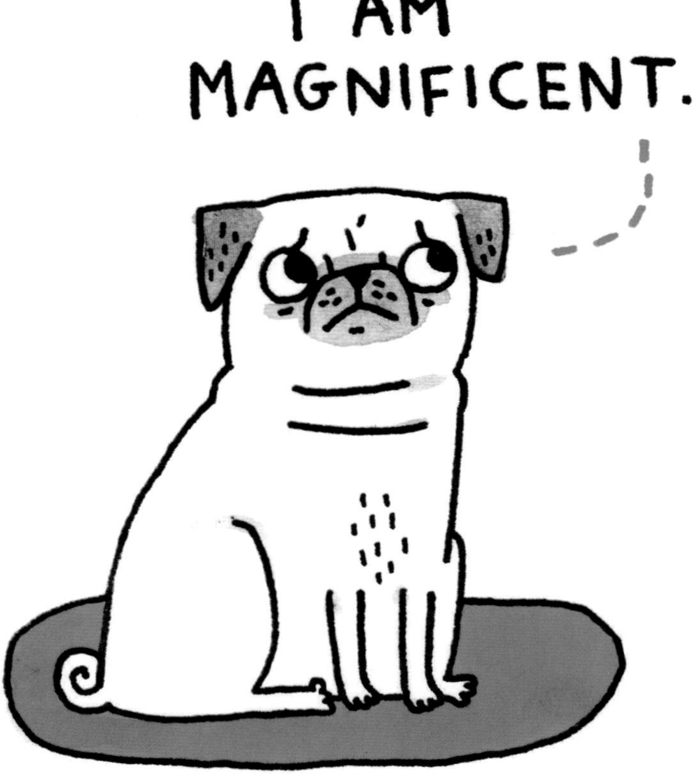
I AM MAGNIFICENT.

# A DOG'S LIFE

## GEMMA CORRELL

**teNeues**

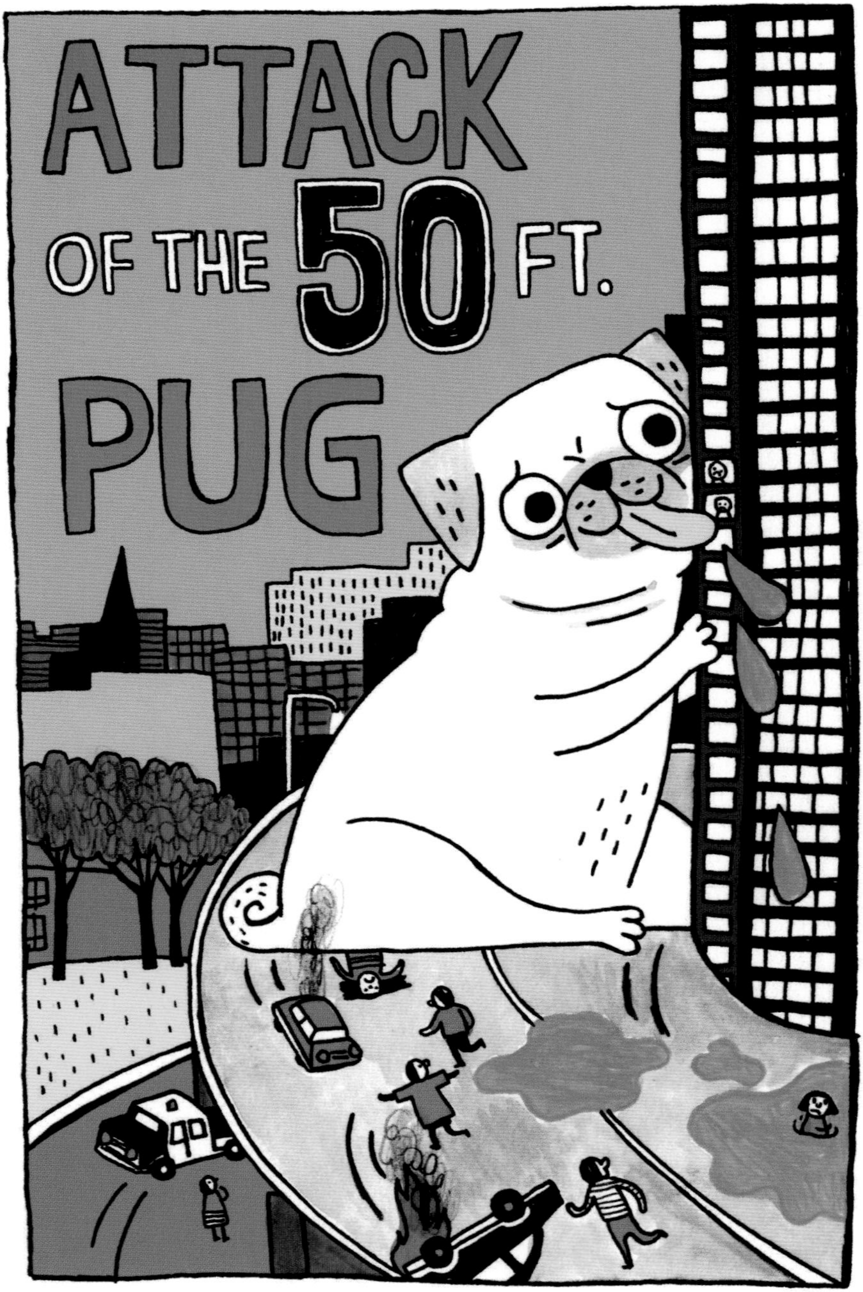
ATTACK
OF THE 50 FT.
PUG

In the world of advertising, fairy tales, and on certain parts of the planet Fantastico Delusionalis, dogs are obedient faithful creatures, who loyally, unswervingly serve their human masters. With glistening coats, mud-free paws, and minty-fresh breath they bound across any hill and dale just to answer their master's call, always willing and responsive to any request, respectfully offering to serve, protect, and obey "their humans." When you're even ever so slightly glum, they'll be there with endearing tricks, wagging tails, and slippers neatly fetched, ready to offer devoted support, respect, and affection. Nowhere in this alternate universe is there any reference to the world most dogs—and their humans—actually do inhabit.

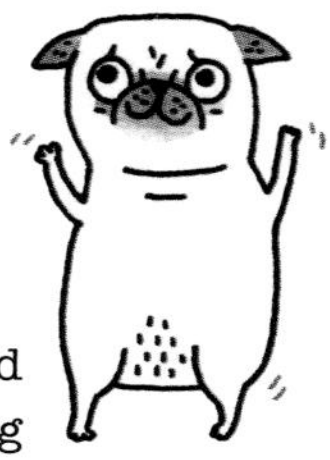

It's this reality that Gemma Correll wryly chronicles in *A Dog's Life*. Browsing through these pages of affectionate yet truthfully rendered vignettes, you'll find yourself nodding in recognition. Ms. Correll's world is one of gnawed chair legs, stale kibble under sofa cushions, and canine glances, which are as much scornful as they are supportive. A world less like that of Lassie and not quite like that of Cujo—somewhere in the mundane middle, if you like.

But that's not to say that dogs aren't incredibly important to us. Quite the contrary! Forget the hunting, protecting, miscellaneous fetching of brandy during avalanches, or rounding up of wayward sheep, these days a dog's main function is to be an entertainer and a clown. No longer just a rare royal privilege, now every household can have its very own jester, whose lively antics, carefree capriciousness, and all-round presence deflects attention from the ever-present parade of bad news in the media, as well as offering welcome distraction from our personal dramas. Who cares if Rover never retrieves a pheasant from a boggy moor, or can't fetch, roll, and beg perfectly on command? So what, if one ear is slightly lopsided and their overall demeanor is more that of a slovenly layabout than a Kennel Club Champion? These woofsters have wooed and won us. In fact, if we put it to a vote, I'd say a substantial number of us would ditch partners, parents, children, and all our worldly goods to sleep in a makeshift shelter with Fido by our side.

Maybe it is their loyalty, and their unaffected insouciance that makes dogs just so incredibly relatable. Could it be that we too would love to give our behinds a good scratch when company comes calling? Who among us hasn't on occasion wanted to jump up and slobber all over an attractive stranger—especially if they have movie-star good looks and might just treat us to a meal? Although we humans might not be too smart, what with our endless wars, working till we drop, and destroying the planet, there's still hope for us....

How about we take a leaf from Fido's book—well from this book actually. Maybe we'd actually benefit from some sofa scratching and chasing a ball around the park for a while? And then, be told how adorable we are? Is this why the Queen of England loves her corgis so? That they just don't stand on ceremony and let her break through all that stifling protocol. Dogs are so much more than man's best friend—they're really a combination of superbly effective therapist, role model, and family member. When you think about it, for the occasional vet's bill, a couple of measly cans of dog food, and daily walks—which keep us fit and get us out of the house—aren't dogs really a harmless, relatively cheap, and all round more sensible alternative to many other modern vices. They are slightly less addictive than drugs, more affectionate than most partners, and way more funny than most of what passes for TV sitcoms these days. From when they first sidled up beside the embers of that Stone Age campfire, put a furry paw and moist snout on our lap, we've been smitten...really, we have. In this game of who's in charge of whom, I'm convinced the score will always be Dogs: 1, Human: 0. Let's just admit that it's high time the whole human race simply rolled over and "played dead"! Whatever way you approach the issue, dogs rule—and they always have.

— Seamus Mullarkey

In der Werbung, in Märchen und bestimmten Bereichen des Planeten Fantastico Delusionalis sind Hunde gehorsame, treue Wesen, die ihren Herren loyal und unbeirrbar dienen. Mit glänzendem Fell, sauberen Pfoten und frischem Atem rennen sie über Hügel und Täler, nur weil. Sie sind immer bereit, zu erfüllen und zu gehorchen und sie bieten ihre Dienste und ihren Schutz mit Ehrerbietung an. Ist man mal etwas bedrückt, stehen sie mit ihren liebenswerten Tricks, wedelnden Schwänzen und herbeigeholten Hausschuhen parat – sie sind stets bereit, ihre Ergebenheit, ihren Respekt und ihre Zuneigung unter Beweis zu stellen. In diesem anderen Universum gibt es keine Bezugnahmen auf die Welt, in der die meisten Hunde – und auch ihre Herren – tatsächlich leben.

Genau diese Umstände hält Gemma Correll in „A Dog's Life" mit trockenem Humor fest. Wenn man durch diese Seiten mit liebevoll, jedoch wahrheitsgemäßen Darstellungen blättert, kann man nur zustimmend nicken. Zu der Welt von Gemma Correll gehören angeknabberte Stuhlbeine, hart gewordene Hundekuchen unter Sofakissen und Blicke, die eher Verachtung als Rückhalt zum Ausdruck bringen. Eine Welt, die nicht ganz der von Lassie gleicht, aber auch nicht so schlimm wie die von Cujo ist.

Man könnte sagen, sie befindet sich irgendwo in der Mitte. Das heißt aber nicht, dass Hunde für uns nicht unglaublich wichtig sind. Ganz im Gegenteil! Jagd- und Schutzfunktionen sowie die Bereithaltung von Cognac bei Lawinenabgängen oder das Einfangen von eigenwilligen Schafen ist nebensächlich – heutzutage sind Hunde hauptsächlich Unterhalter und Clowns. Schon lange ist dies kein Vorrecht des Adels mehr. Jetzt kann sich jeder Haushalt seinen eigenen Hofnarren halten, durch dessen lebhafte Possen, sorglos kapriziöses Verhalten und Omnipräsenz wir die ständige Flut schlechter Nachrichtenmeldungen vorübergehend vergessen und die eine willkommene Ablenkung von unseren persönlichen Dramen bieten. Wen interessiert es schon, ob Rolf jemals einen aus einem sumpfigen Moor apportiert hat oder auf Befehl nicht perfekt fangen, überrollen oder betteln

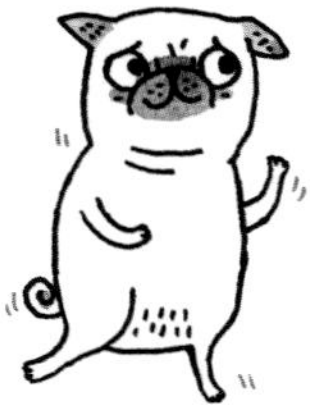

kann? Und was ist schon dabei, wenn ein Ohr ein bisschen schief ist und das Benehmen insgesamt mehr dem verlotterten Nichtstuers als dem eines Kennel Club-Siegers gleicht? Diese Vierbeiner haben uns für sich vereinnahmt. Wenn wir eine Abstimmung durchführen würden, würde ich, dass viele von uns Partner, Eltern, Kinder und gesamte weltliche Habe hinter uns lassen würden, um mit an Seite in einer improvisierten Herberge zu schlafen.

Vielleicht ist es ihre Loyalität oder ihre unaffektierte Unbekümmertheit, wodurch wir uns so stark zu Hunden hingezogen fühlen. Könnte es sein, dass wir uns in Gegenwart von Gästen auch gerne ungeniert am Hinterteil kratzen würden? Wer wäre nicht schon mal gerne an einem attraktiven Fremden hochgesprungen, um ihn abzuküssen, insbesondere wenn der- oder diejenige wie ein Filmstar aussieht und uns vielleicht zum Essen einlädt? Obwohl wir Menschen nicht allzu klug sind, was wir durch unsere endlosen Kriege, langen und ermüdenden Arbeitsstunden und die Zerstörung unserer Erde immer wieder unter Beweis stellen, gibt es für uns dennoch Hoffnung.

Wie wäre es, wenn wir uns von oder besser gesagt von diesem Buch eine Scheibe abschneiden würden? Vielleicht wäre es nur zu unserem Vorteil, wenn wir das Sofa ein bisschen zerkratzen oder im Park einem Ball hinterherjagen würden, um dann gesagt zu bekommen, wie bezaubernd wir sind? Ist dies der Grund dafür, warum die englische Königin ihre Corgis so liebt? Dass ihnen Feierlichkeiten gleichgültig sind und ihr erlauben, sich aus dem Zwang des Protokolls zu befreien? Hunde sind viel, viel mehr als der beste Freund des Menschen. Sie sind eine meisterhafte Mischung aus einem guten Therapeuten, einem Vorbild und einem Familienmitglied. Abgesehen von gelegentlichen Tierarztrechnungen, ein paar Dosen Hundefutter und täglichen Spaziergängen, die uns fit halten und wodurch wir aus dem Haus kommen, sind Hunde – wenn man sich das richtig überlegt - wirklich eine harmlose, relativ billige und insgesamt viel vernünftigere Alternative zu manch anderen modernen Lastern. Sie machen etwas weniger süchtig als Drogen, sie sind liebevoller als die meisten Partner und unterhaltsamer als das, was heute als Sitcoms im Fernsehen läuft.

— Seamus Mullarkey

# Dans le <sup></sup>monde de la publicité, des contes de fées et dans certains endroits de la planète

Fantastico Delusionalis, les chiens sont des créatures fidèles et obéissantes qui servent avec loyauté leurs maitres humains et leurs sont dévoués corps et âme. Ils ont des pelages brillants, des pattes sans une trace de boue, une halène fraiche et mentholée et ils sont prêts à courir par monts et par vaux juste pour répondre à l'appel de leur maître, toujours prêts et heureux de satisfaire toutes les demandes en offrant respectueusement de servir, protéger et obéir « à leurs humains. » Lorsque vous êtes d'une humeur même légèrement maussade, ils sont là avec des tours de passe-passe charmants, la queue battante et des pantoufles proprement présentées, prêts à offrir un appui dévoué avec respect et affection. Nulle part dans cet univers alternatif il ne sera fait référence au monde où vivent en réalité la plupart des chiens, et leurs humains.

C'est précisément cette réalité que Gemma Correll décrit avec ironie dans « Une vie de chien. » En feuilletant ces pages avec des vignettes pleines de tendresse mais aussi très vraies vous allez hocher la tête en signe d'approbation. L'univers de Mme Correll est celui où les pieds des chaises sont rongés, avec des bouts de croquettes rancies sous les coussins du canapé et des regards canins qui semblent plutôt vous reprocher quelque chose au lieu de vous appuyer. Un univers qui est bien moins celui de Lassie et pas tout à fait celui de Cujo. Quelque part au milieu si vous voulez. Mais ceci ne veut pas dire que les chiens ne soient pas incroyablement importants pour nous. Bien au contraire ! Oubliez la chasse, la garde et le tonnelet de rhum qui vous est présenté pendant les avalanches ou bien les brebis égarées qui sont ramenées dans le troupeau, de nos jours le rôle principal du chien c'est d'être un artiste et un clown. Il ne s'agit plus d'un privilège royal, maintenant chaque foyer peut avoir son bouffon, dont les pitreries, les caprices insouciants et la seule présence nous permettent de ne plus accorder d'attention au défilé incessant de mauvaises nouvelles dans les médias, tout en nous offrant une distraction pour oublier nos tragédies personnelles. Peu importe que notre toutou ne retrouvera jamais un faisan dans un marécage ou qu'il ne sache pas rapporter, se rouler par terre et quémander parfaitement sur commande. Et qu'est-ce que ça peut nous faire si une oreille est légèrement déformée et que dans l'ensemble son comportement serait plutôt celui d'un fainéant désinvolte que celui d'un champion du Club Canin ? Ces doux aboyeurs nous ont courtisés et séduits. En fait s'il fallait voter, je dirais qu'un nombre substantiel parmi nous, serait prêt à délaisser leur partenaire, leurs parents, leurs enfants et tous les biens de ce monde pour dormir dans un abri de fortune avec leur toutou.

C'est peut-être leur loyauté et leur insouciance naturelle qui rendent les chiens tellement incroyablement irrésistibles et proches de nous. Se pourrait-il que nous aussi nous aimerions bien nous gratter le derrière à l'aise lorsque nous avons des invités ? Qui parmi nous n'a pas voulu parfois sauter en bavant partout sur un inconnu plein d'attrait et tout particulièrement s'il est beau comme un acteur de cinéma et peut même nous inviter à diner ? Bien que nous les humains nous ne soyons peut-être pas très intelligents, voyez nos guerres incessantes, le travail jusqu'à en tomber d'épuisement et la destruction de la planète, il y a encore un espoir pour nous ...

Pourquoi ne pas prendre une page du livre de notre toutou, en fait ce livre que vous lisez. Peut-être que nous pourrions profiter de gratter le canapé et de pourchasser une balle à travers le parc pendant un moment ? Et puis quelqu'un nous dira que nous sommes adorables ? Est-ce pour cette raison que la Reine d'Angleterre aime tellement ses corgis ? Le fait qu'ils ne peuvent pas rester tranquilles pendant les cérémonies et lui donnent l'occasion de faire une entorse à ce protocole étouffant ? Les chiens sont bien plus que le meilleur ami de l'homme, ils sont réellement tout à la fois un psychologue superbement efficace, un modèle à suivre et un membre de la famille. Tout compte fait, avec de temps en temps une facture du vétérinaire, quelques petites boites de nourriture pour chiens et des promenades quotidiennes qui nous conservent en pleine forme et nous font sortir de la maison, les chiens ne sont-ils pas une alternative sans danger, relativement bon marché et en tout et pour tout beaucoup plus censée que de nombreux vices modernes ? Ils provoquent légèrement moins de dépendance que la drogue, ils sont plus affectueux que la plupart des partenaires et bien plus drôles que les prétendues comédies que vous voyez de nos jours à la télévision. Du temps où ils se sont joints à nous près des braises du feu de camp pendant cet âge de pierre, en mettant une patte poilue et un museau humide sur nos genoux nous sommes sous le charme. Vraiment ... Dans ce jeu de qui commande, je suis convaincu que le score sera toujours Chiens : 1 Humain : 0. Admettons-le, il est grand temps que toute la race humaine se couche pour « faire le mort ». Quelle que soit notre approche sur ce point, les chiens règnent en maître et ce depuis toujours.

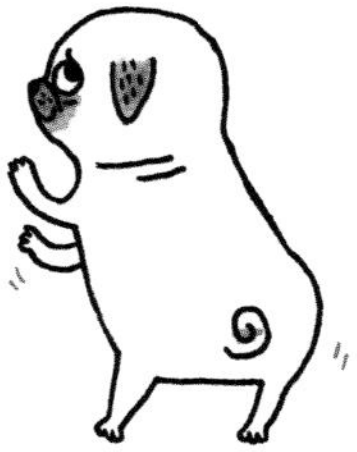

— Seamus Mullarkey

# DOG CARE ONE OH ONE

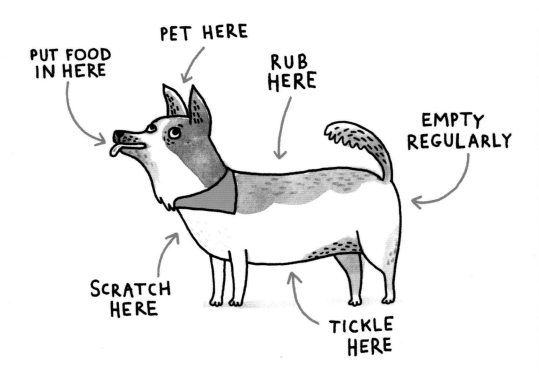

PUT FOOD IN HERE

PET HERE

RUB HERE

EMPTY REGULARLY

SCRATCH HERE

TICKLE HERE

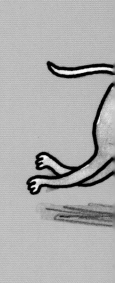

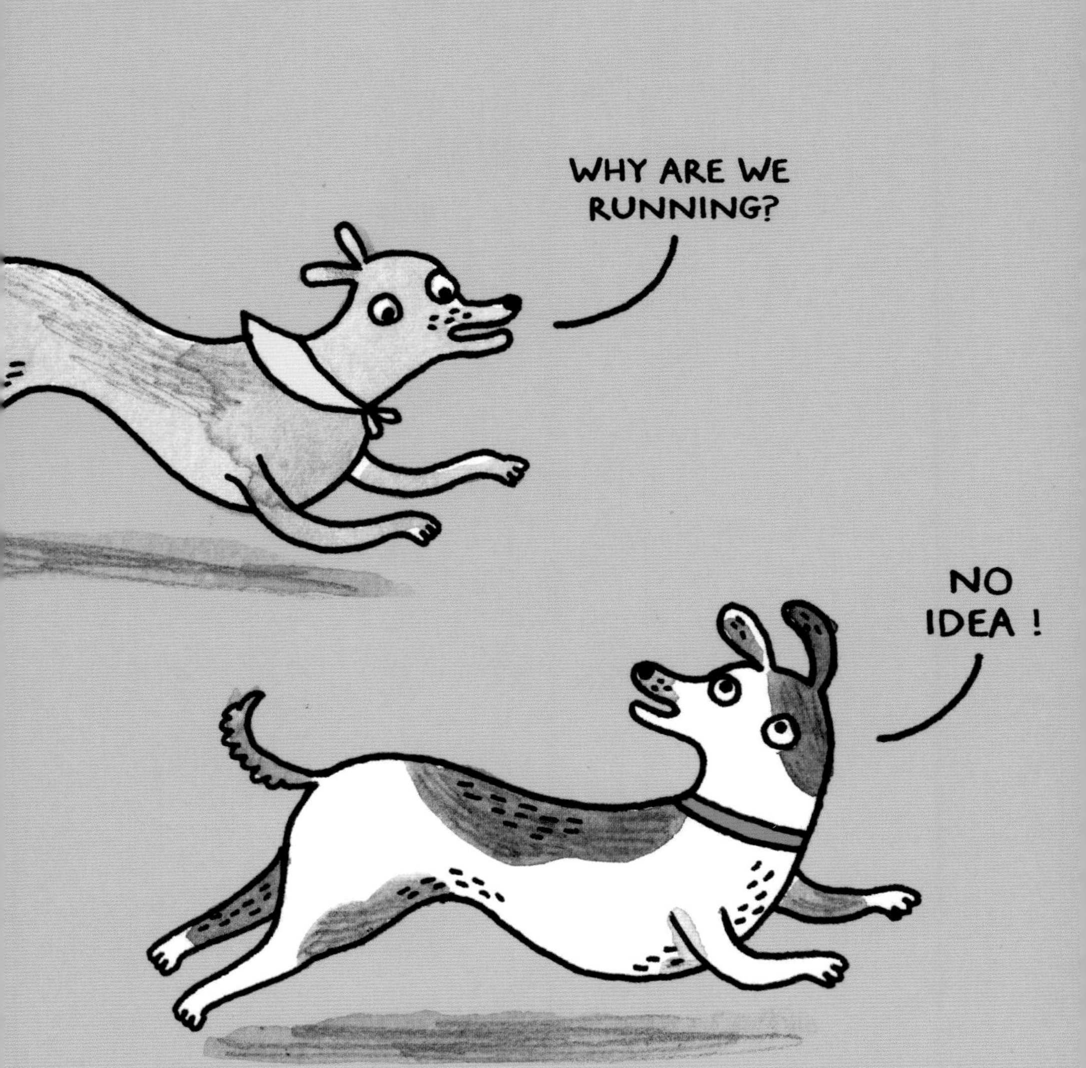
WHY ARE WE RUNNING?
NO IDEA !

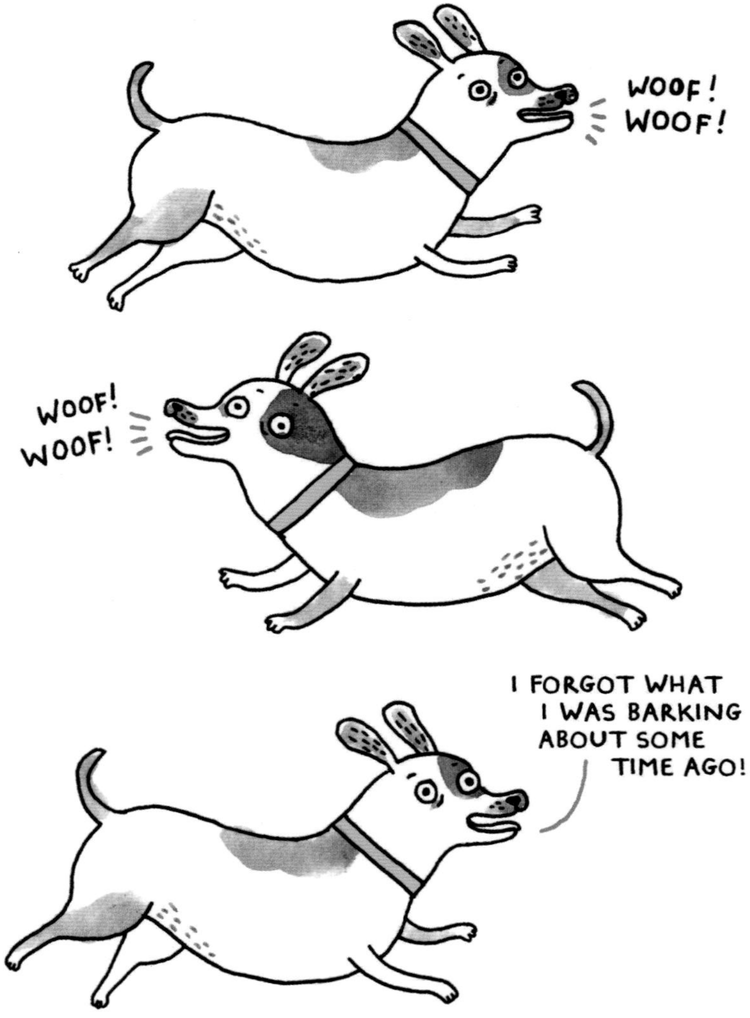
WOOF! WOOF!
WOOF! WOOF!
I FORGOT WHAT I WAS BARKING ABOUT SOME TIME AGO!

# DOGGY CONFESSION TIME

I LICK MY BUTT AND
THEN LICK YOUR FACE

I DRINK OUT
OF THE TOILET

I PEED IN YOUR
ORNAMENTAL GARDEN

THE CAT AND I
ARE IN CAHOOTS

I WATCH YOU
SHOWER

I KNOW WHAT
HAPPENED TO YOUR
MISSING SHOE ...

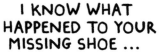

THE OLD GOOD PUP/BAD PUP ROUTINE

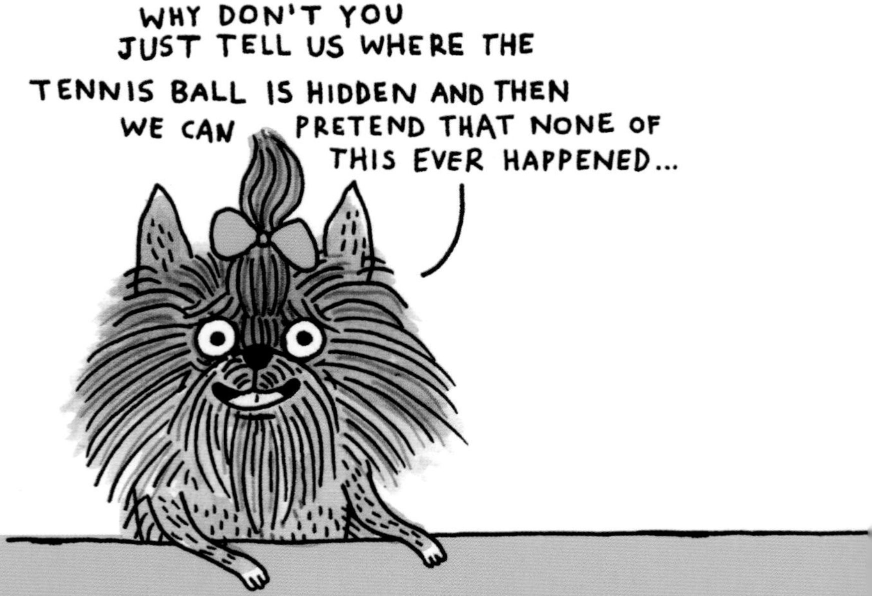
WHY DON'T YOU JUST TELL US WHERE THE TENNIS BALL IS HIDDEN AND THEN WE CAN PRETEND THAT NONE OF THIS EVER HAPPENED...

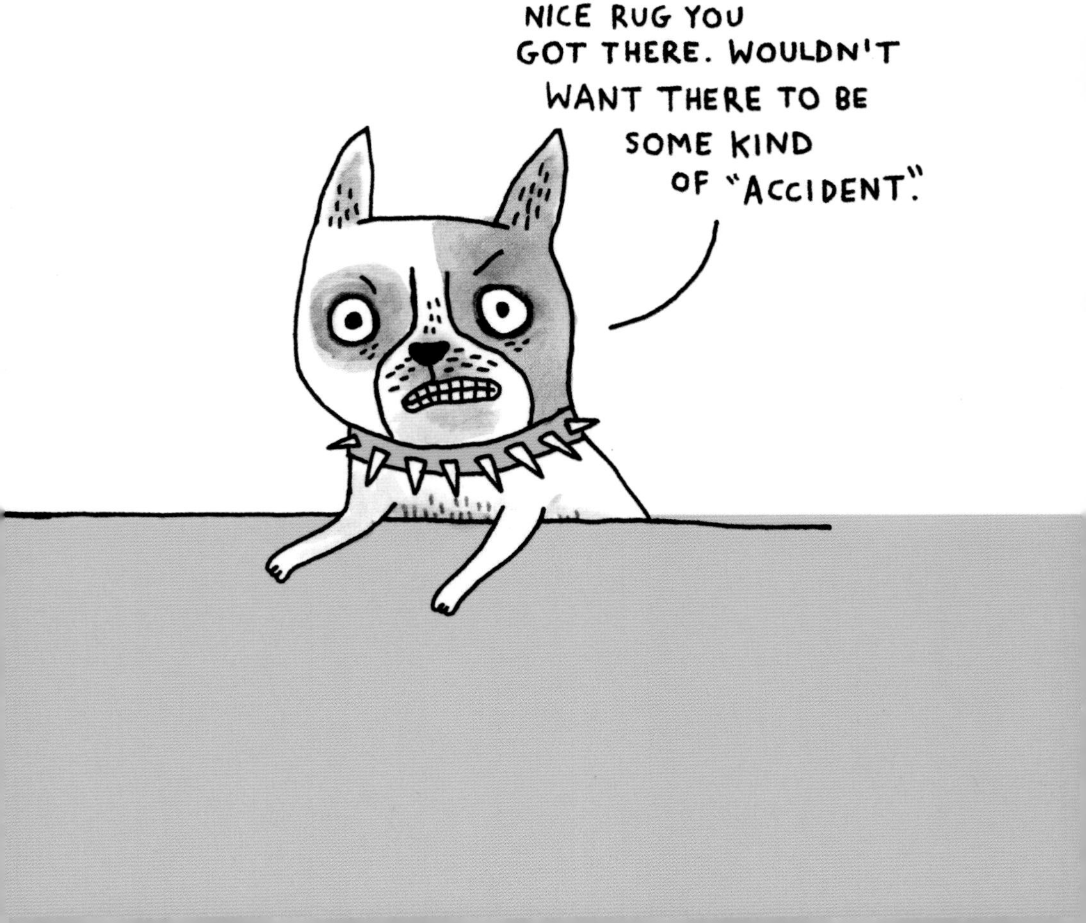
NICE RUG YOU GOT THERE. WOULDN'T WANT THERE TO BE SOME KIND OF "ACCIDENT."

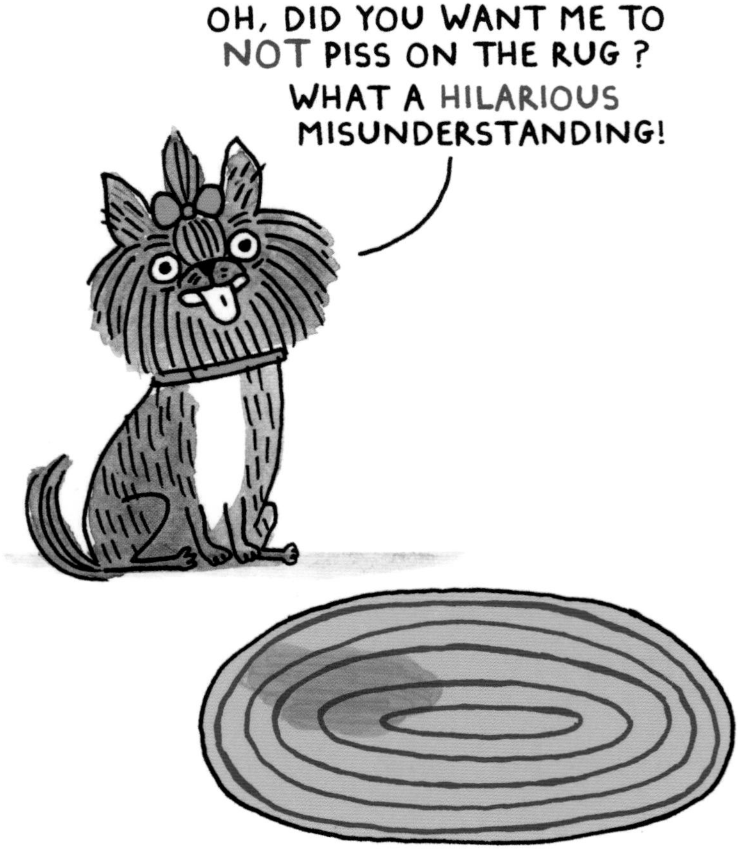
OH, DID YOU WANT ME TO NOT PISS ON THE RUG ? WHAT A HILARIOUS MISUNDERSTANDING!

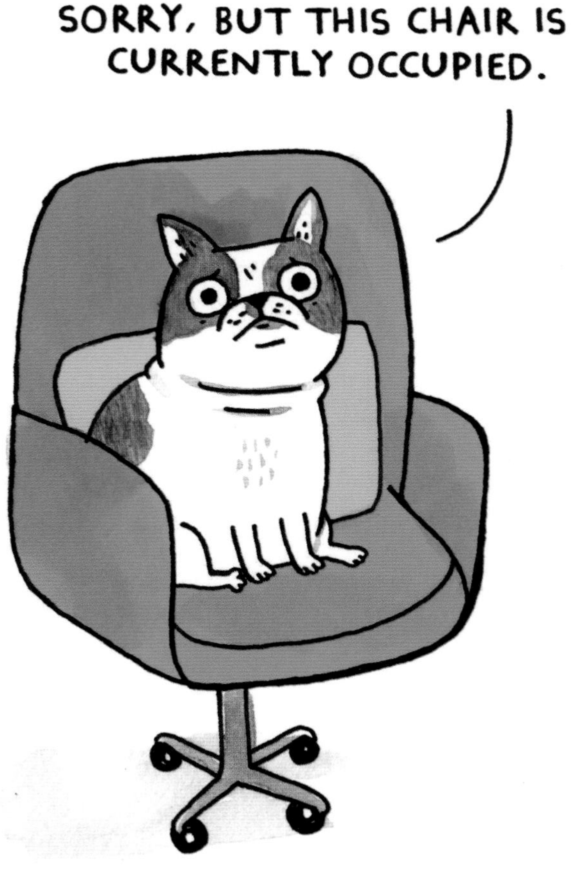
SORRY, BUT THIS CHAIR IS CURRENTLY OCCUPIED.

# THE ETERNAL DILEMMA

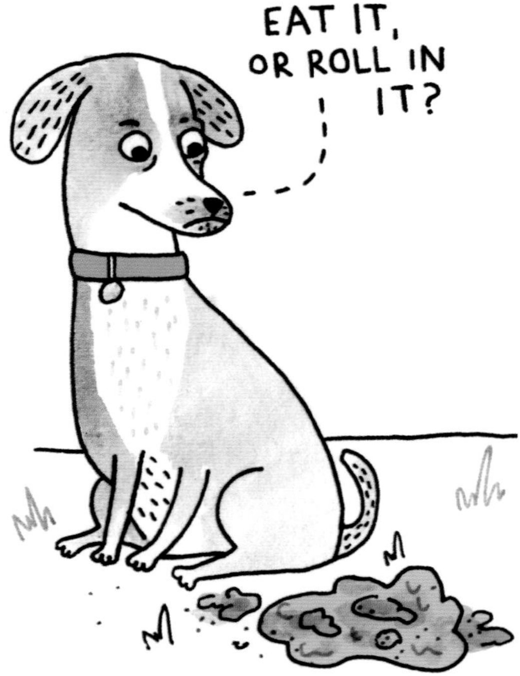
EAT IT, OR ROLL IN IT?

LET SLEEPING DOGS LIE

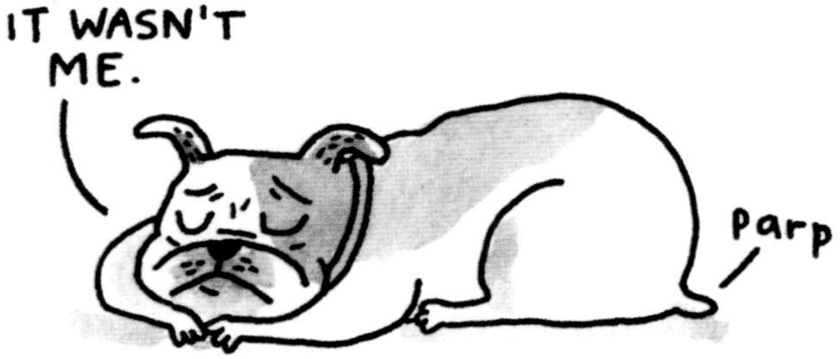
IT WASN'T ME.
parp

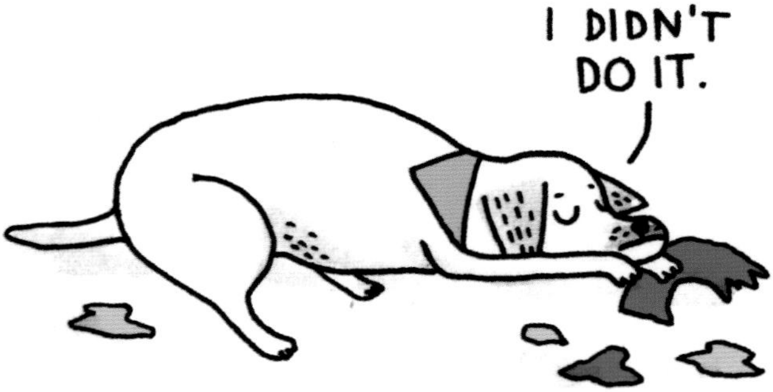
I DIDN'T DO IT.

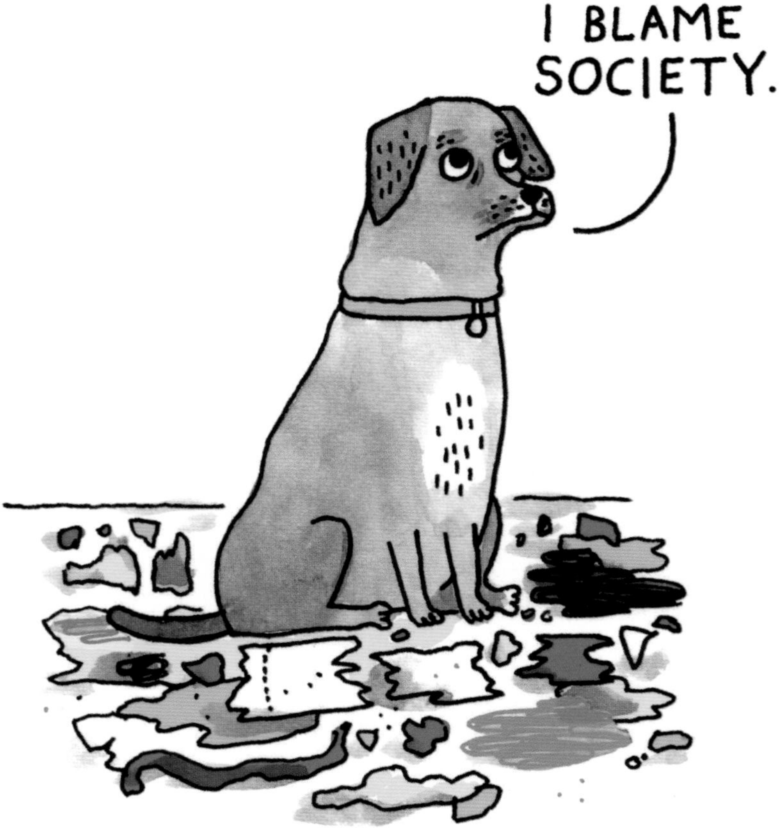
I BLAME SOCIETY.

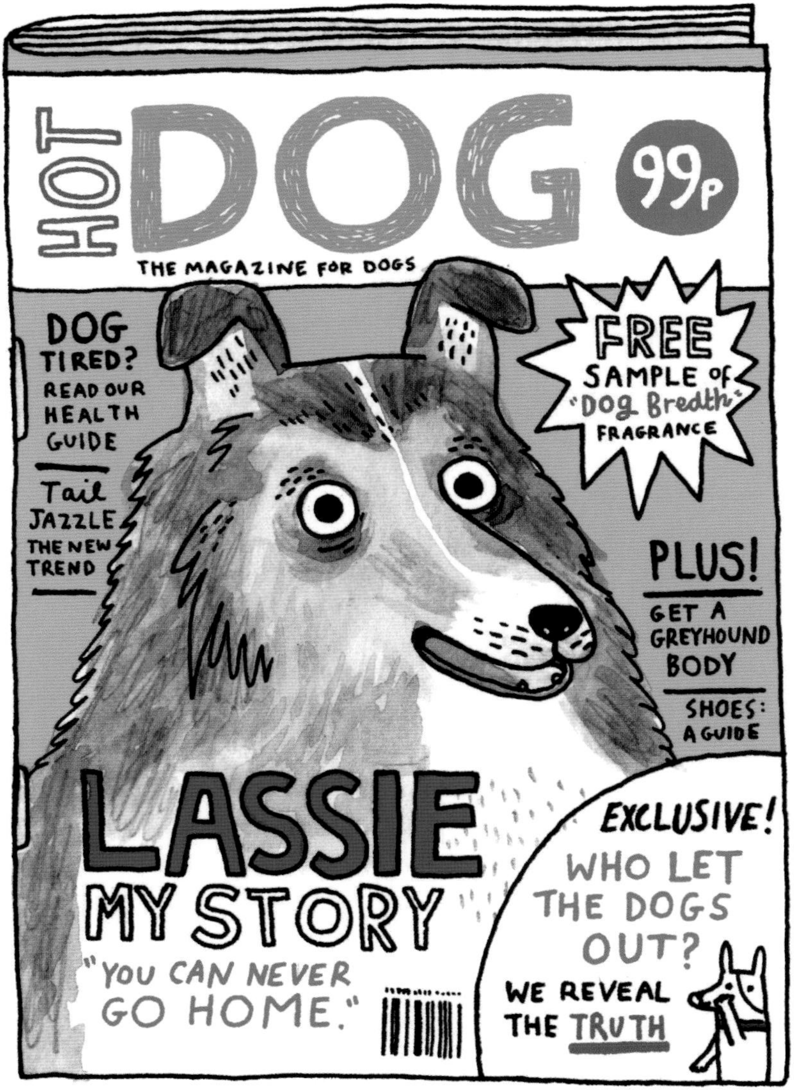
HOT DOG
99p
THE MAGAZINE FOR DOGS
DOG TIRED? READ OUR HEALTH GUIDE
Tail JAZZLE THE NEW TREND
FREE SAMPLE OF "Dog Bredth" FRAGRANCE
PLUS!
GET A GREYHOUND BODY
SHOES: A GUIDE
LASSIE MY STORY
"YOU CAN NEVER GO HOME."
EXCLUSIVE!
WHO LET THE DOGS OUT?
WE REVEAL THE TRUTH

**SPEAK**
NO EVIL

**SEE**
NO EVIL

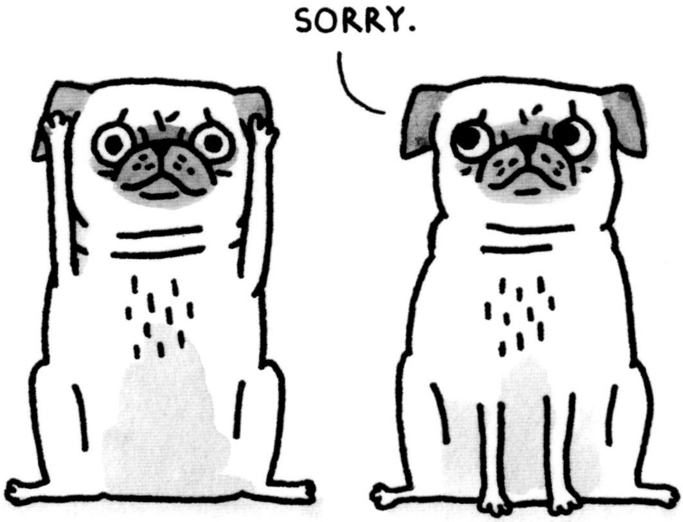
SORRY.

HEAR
NO EVIL

SMELL
NO EVIL

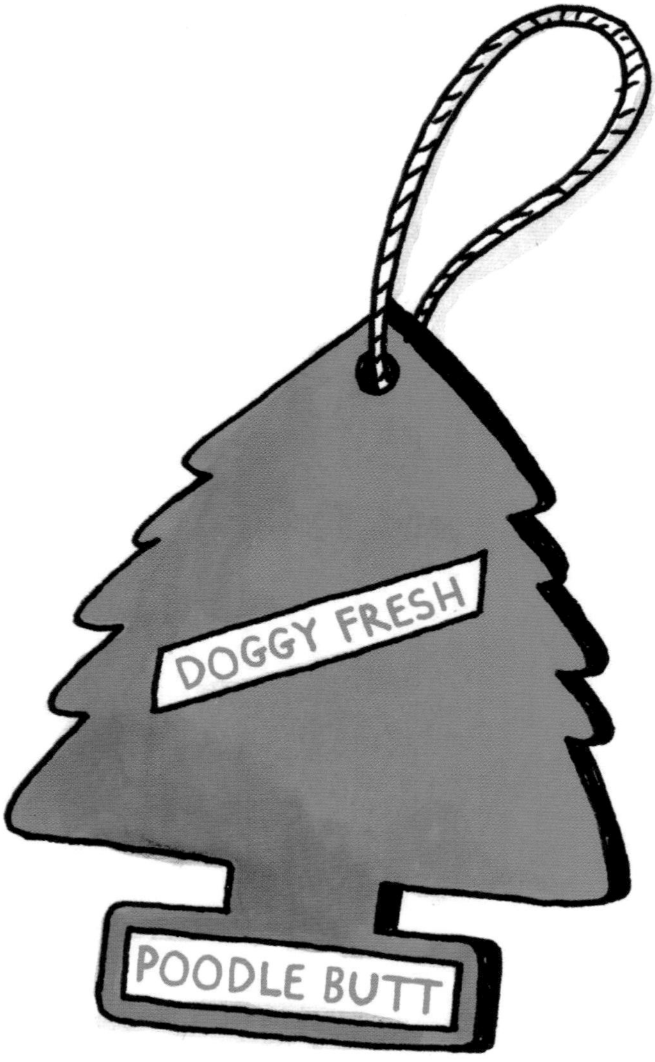
DOGGY FRESH
POODLE BUTT

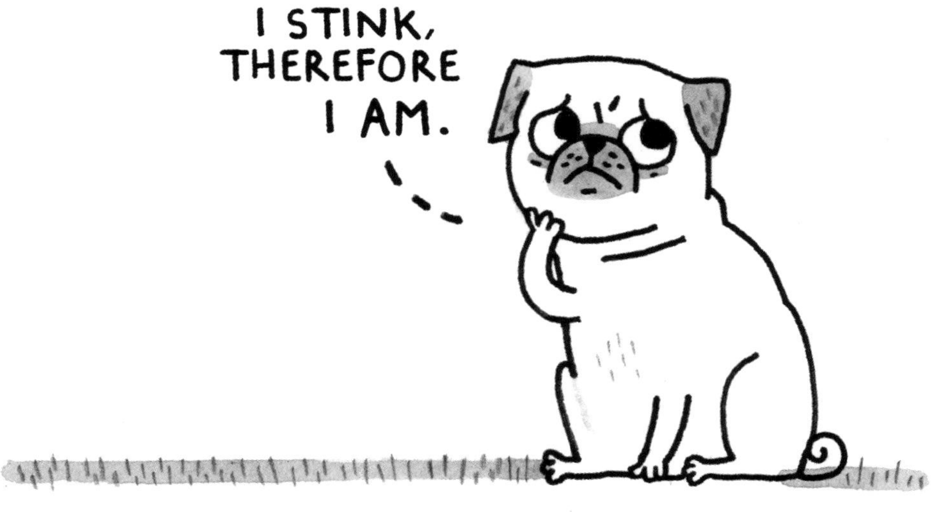
I STINK,
THEREFORE
I AM.

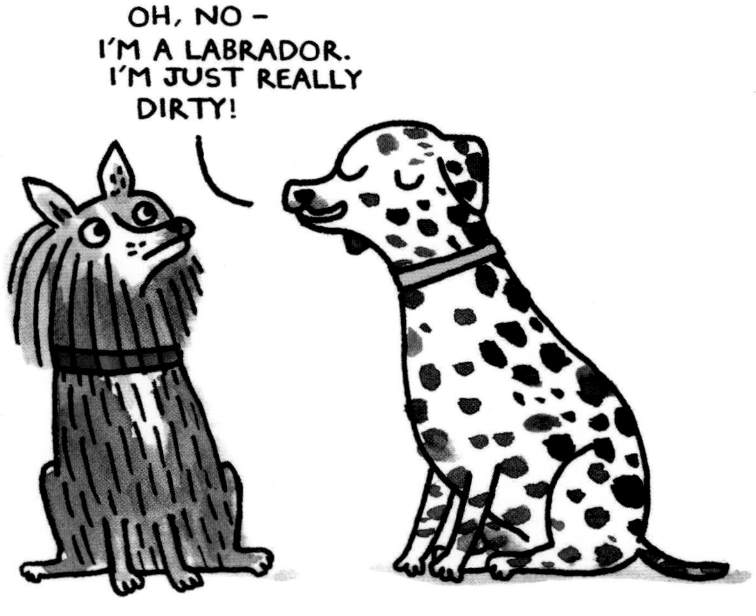
OH, NO –
I'M A LABRADOR.
I'M JUST REALLY
DIRTY!

THAT THING YOU'RE TRYING TO TEACH ME ? I ALREADY KNOW HOW TO DO IT. I JUST ENJOY WATCHING YOU SQUIRM.

# OLD DOGS, NEW TRICKS

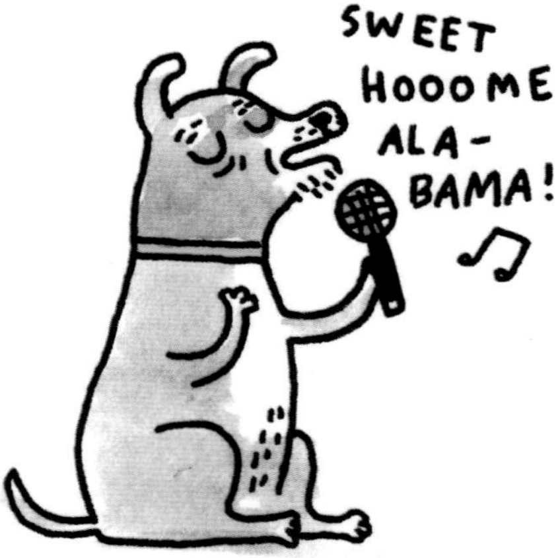
SWEET
HOOOME
ALA-
BAMA!

KARAOKE

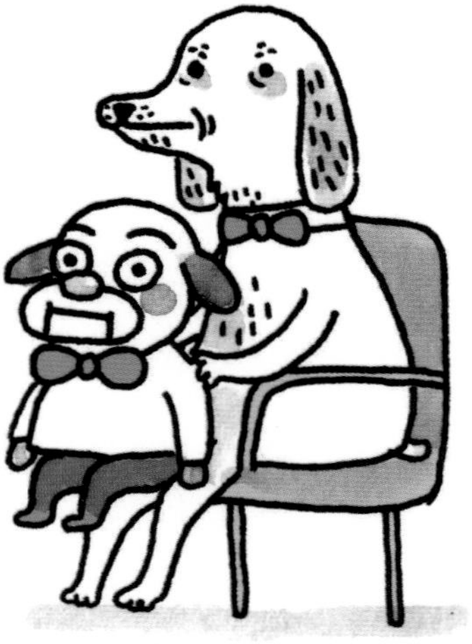

VENTRILOQUISM

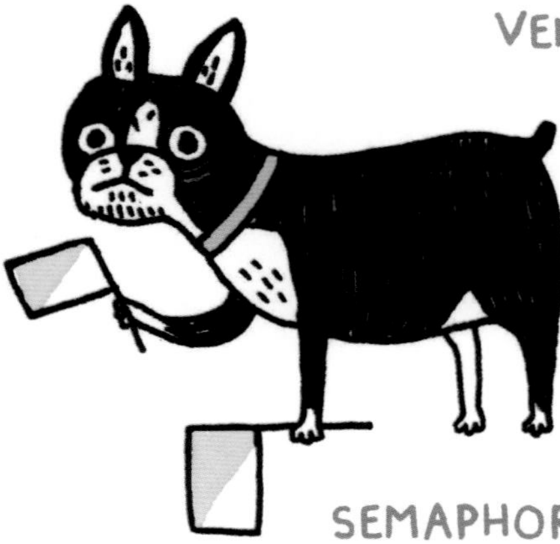

SEMAPHORE

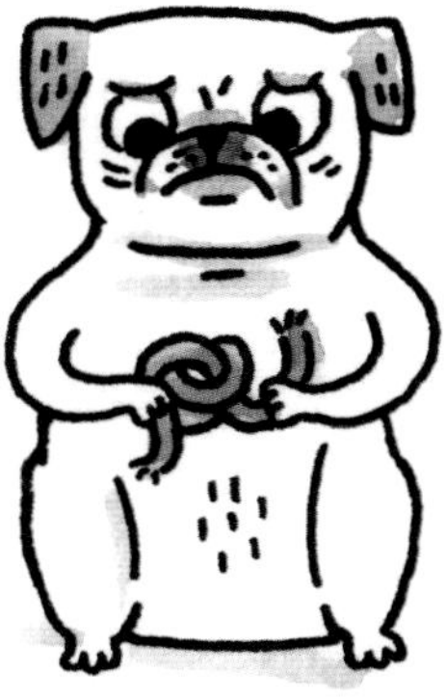

KNOT TYING

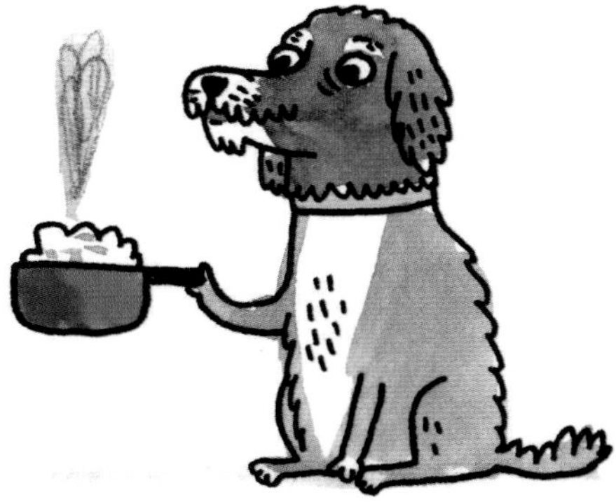

LATVIAN COOKERY

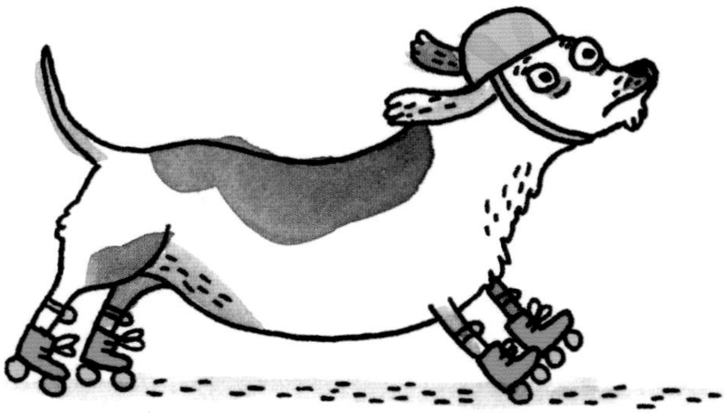

ROLLERSKATING

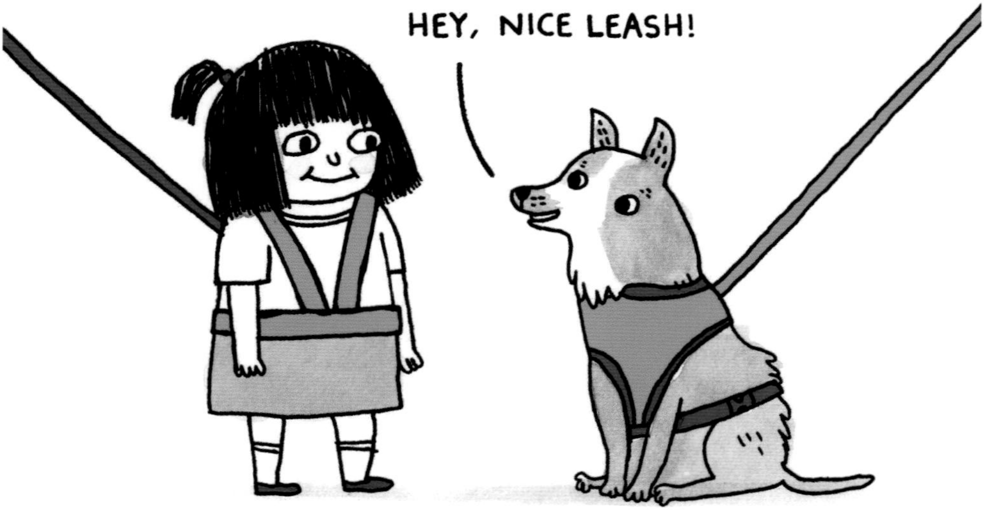
HEY, NICE LEASH!

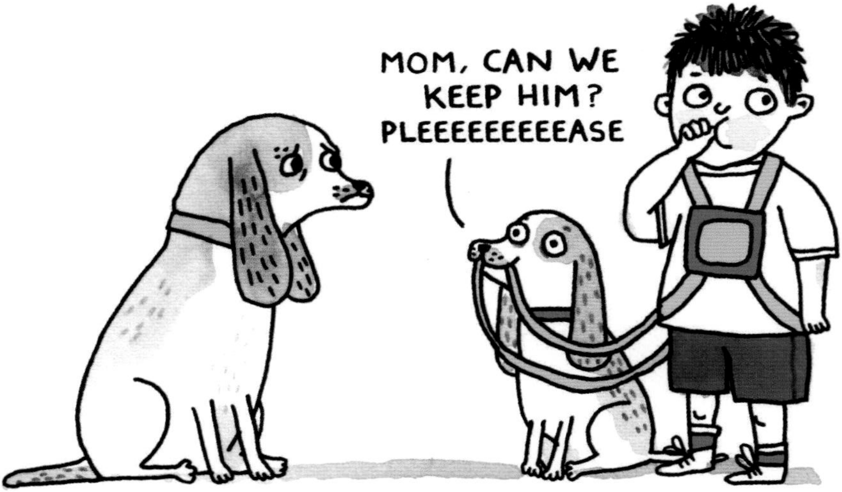
MOM, CAN WE
KEEP HIM?
PLEEEEEEEEEASE

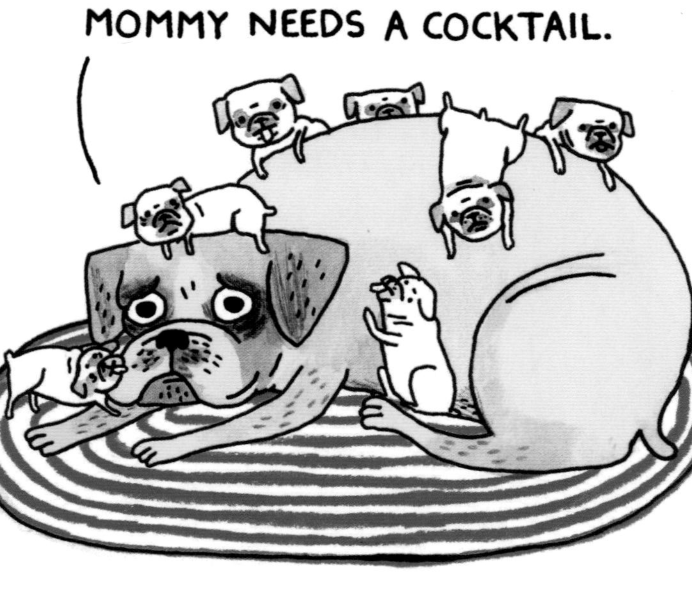
MOMMY NEEDS A COCKTAIL.

# DOG BREEDS OF THE WORLD

AUSTRALIAN TERRIER

ITALIAN GREYHOUND

SWEDISH SHOE CHEWER

ENGLISH SPANIEL

FRENCH BULLDOG

CANADIAN BUTT LICKER

GERMAN SHEPHERD

parp

VENEZUELAN FARTER

CHIA—HUAHUA

**TEACUP
CHIHUAHUA**

**EGGCUP
CHIHUAHUA**

**TEASPOON
CHIHUAHUA**

**THIMBLE
CHIHUAHUA**

**PINHEAD
CHIHUAHUA**

**SUBATOMIC
PARTICLE
CHIHUAHUA**

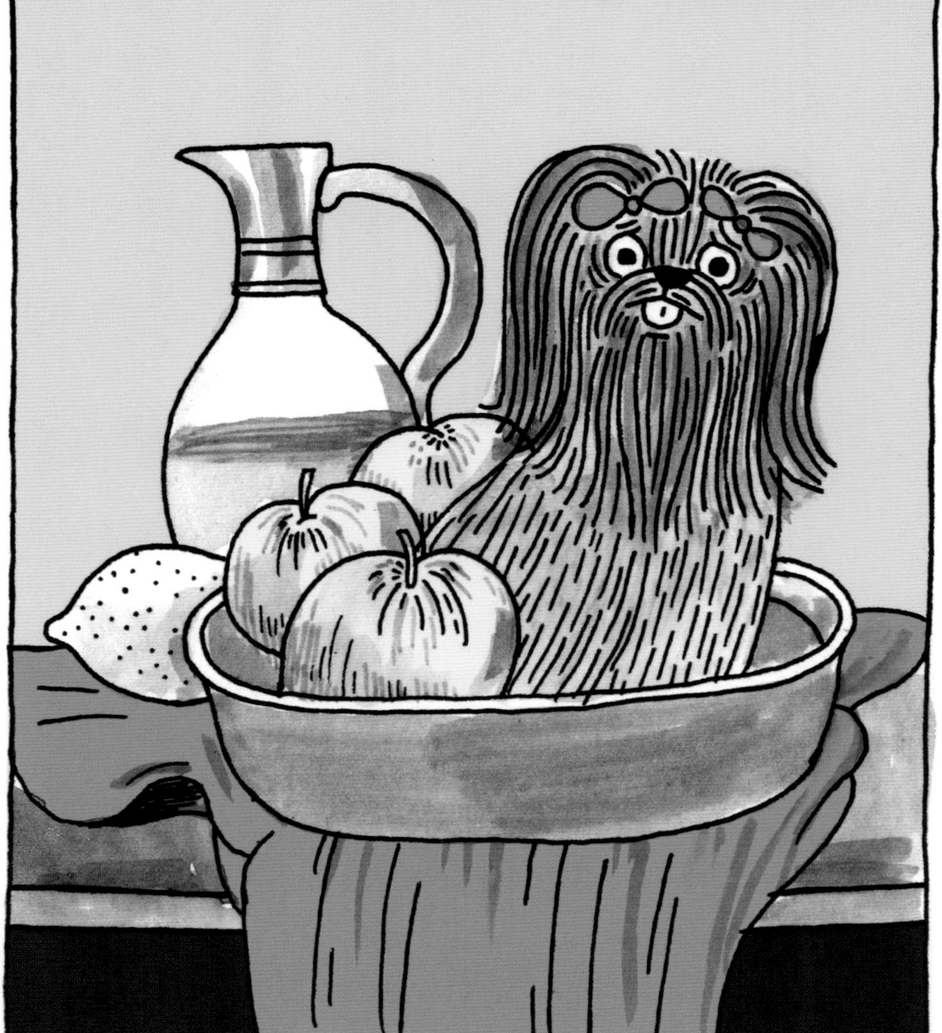

"Still life with Shih-Tzu"

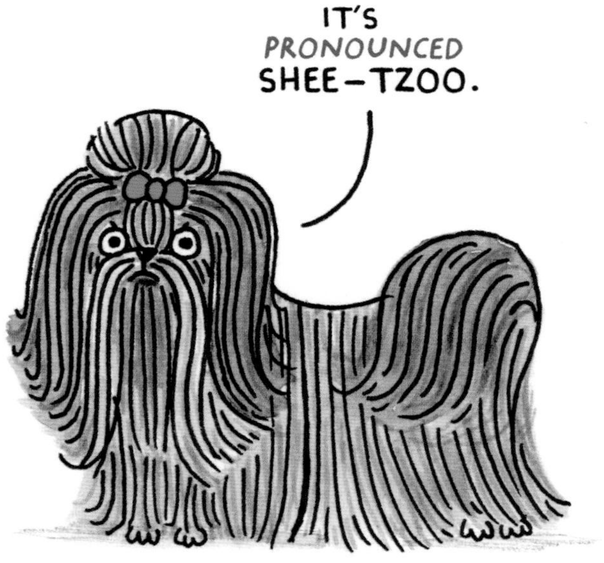
IT'S PRONOUNCED SHEE-TZOO.

LUMBER JACK RUSSELL

# LEGENDS OF CANINEDOM

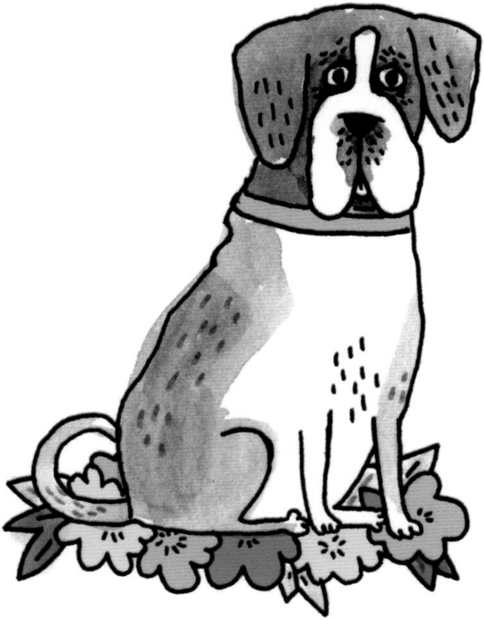

## ST. BERNARD

HEROICALLY RESCUED A GROUP OF YOUNG PUPPIES WHO HAD BECOME TRAPPED BEHIND A COUCH BY A PARTICULARLY NOISY VACUUM CLEANER

## SIR. FLUFFINTON OF BOSTON
LED THE 24th SMUSH-FACED BATTALION TO
VICTORY AT THE BATTLE OF MANGY SOCK, 2012

## DR. WIENER, P.H.D.
TREATED DOGS DURING THE GREAT GRAVY BONE
FAMINE OF '09, IN WHICH THOUSANDS OF
POOCHES WERE FORCED TO GO WITHOUT TASTY
MEAT-BASED TREATS FOR ALMOST 24 HOURS.

## MIXED BREEDS

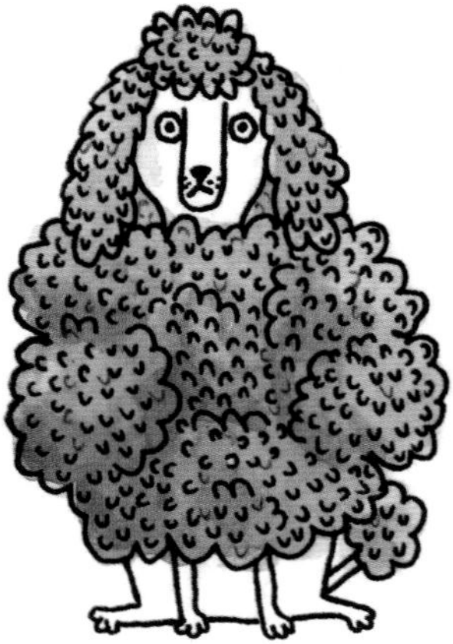

POODOCCOLI

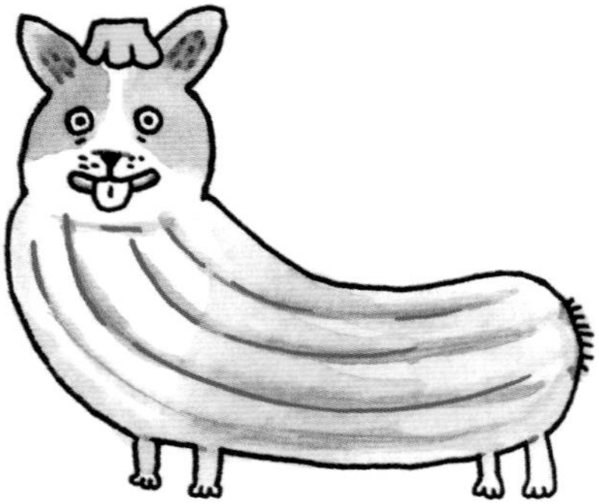

CORGETTE

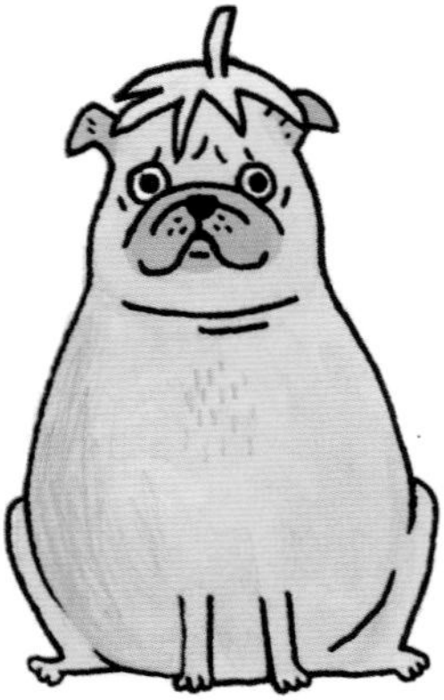

BULLBERGINE

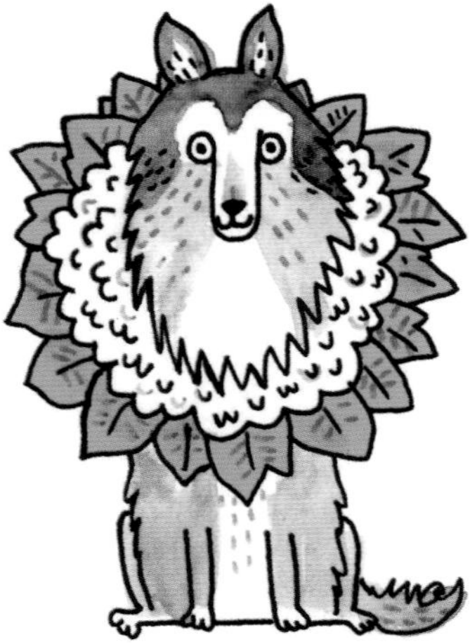

COLLIEFLOWER

KALEHOUND

THE ANCIENT POODLE TRIBE OF
NORTHERN FRANCE HUNT FOR KIBBLE

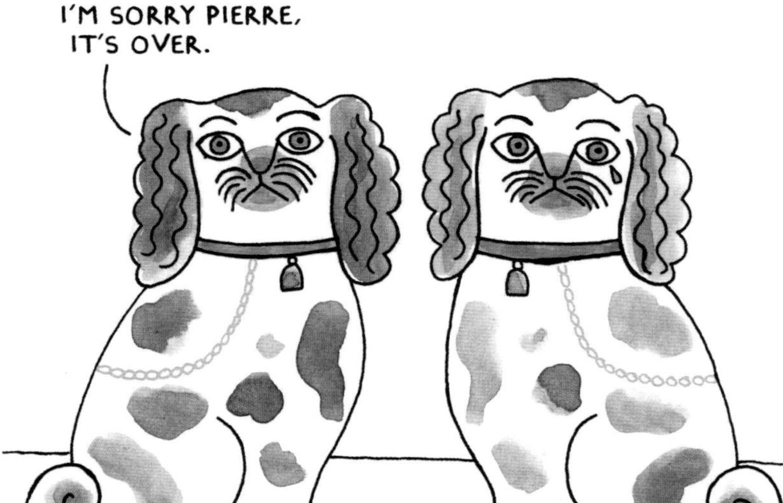
I'M SORRY PIERRE,
IT'S OVER.

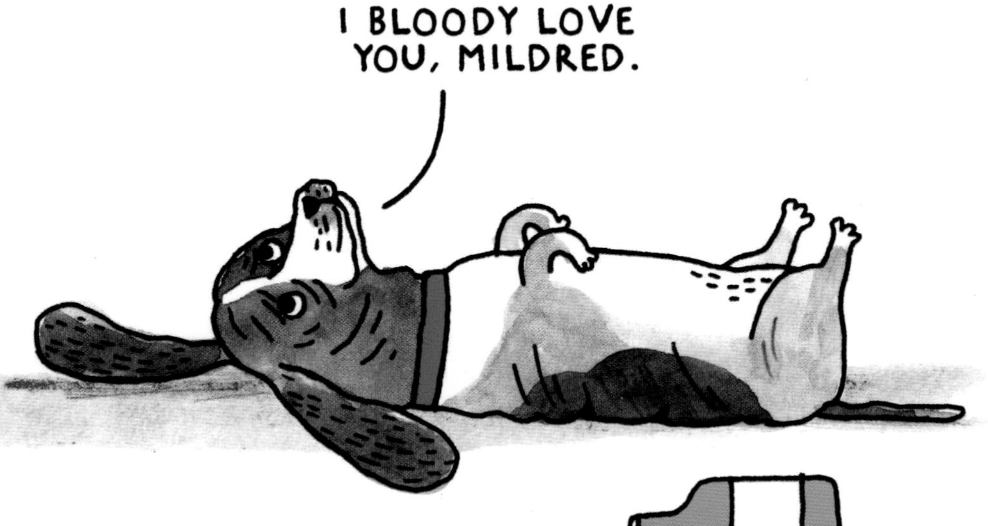
I BLOODY LOVE YOU, MILDRED.

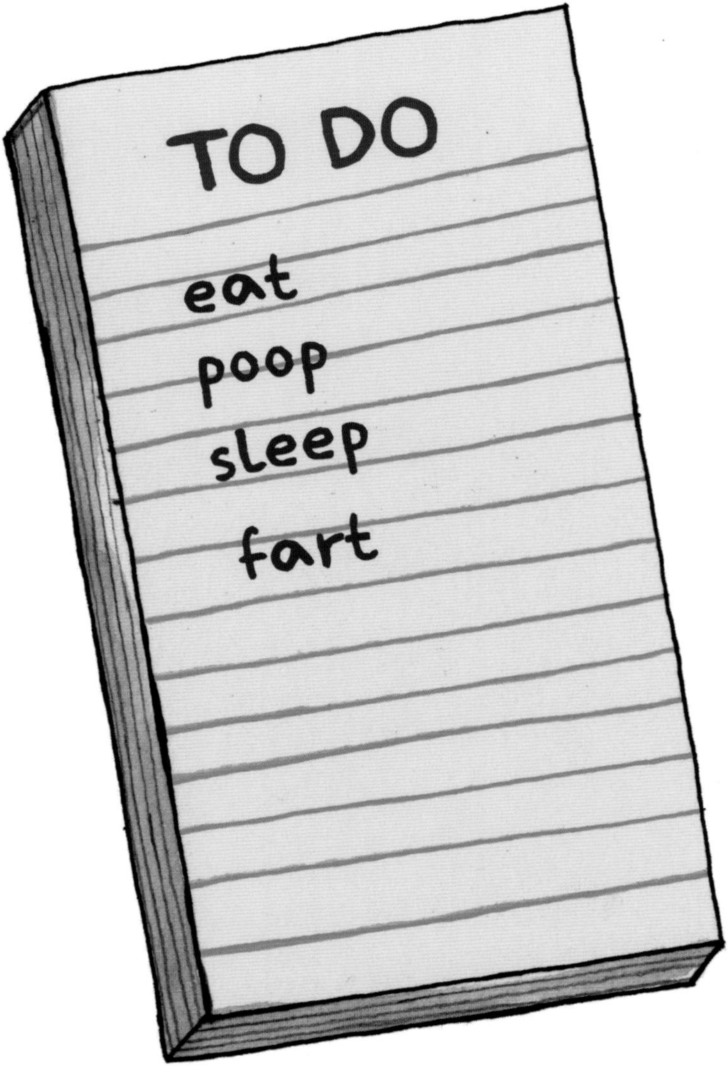
TO DO
eat
poop
sleep
fart

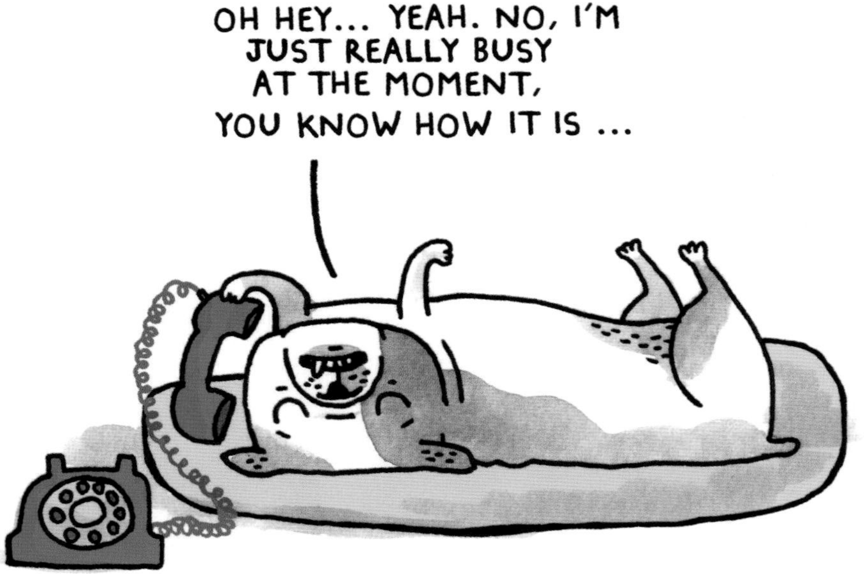
OH HEY... YEAH. NO, I'M JUST REALLY BUSY AT THE MOMENT, YOU KNOW HOW IT IS ...

THE CALL OF THE WILD

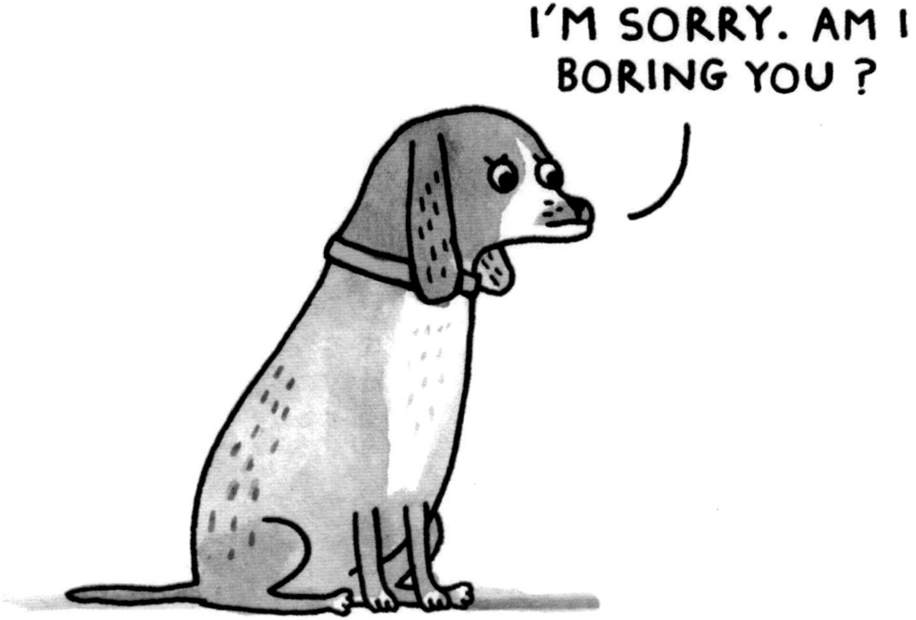
I'M SORRY. AM I
BORING YOU ?

YEP.

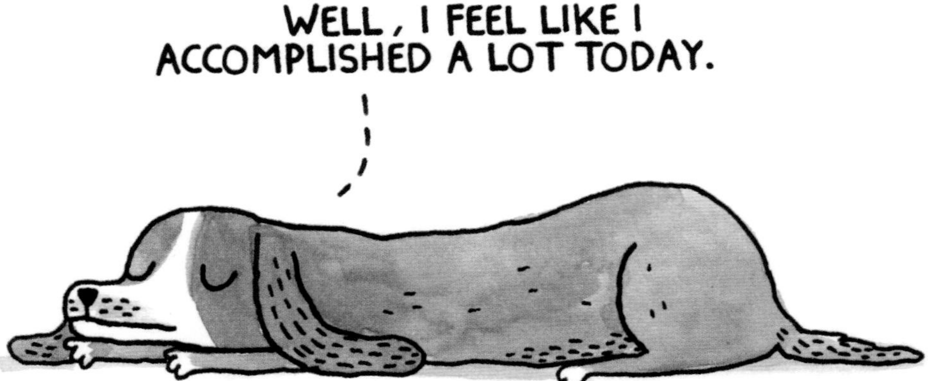
WELL, I FEEL LIKE I ACCOMPLISHED A LOT TODAY.

I WONDER
WHAT'S
FOR DINNER ...

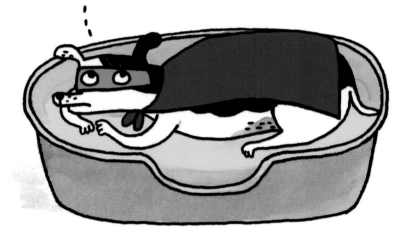

REX , THE WONDER DOG

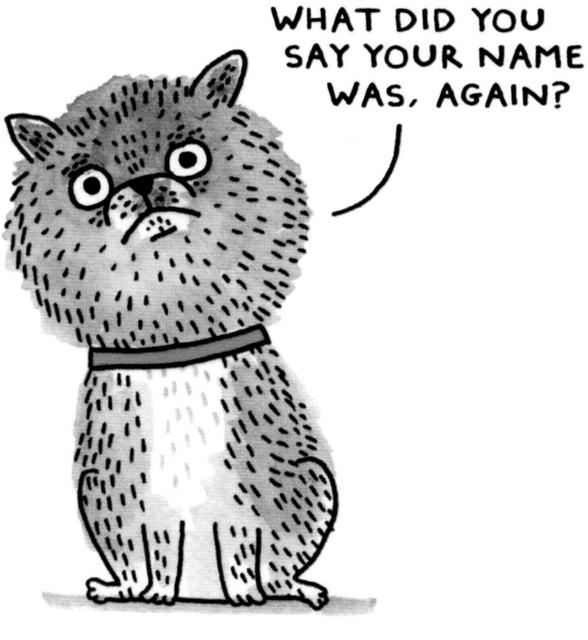
WHAT DID YOU
SAY YOUR NAME
WAS, AGAIN?

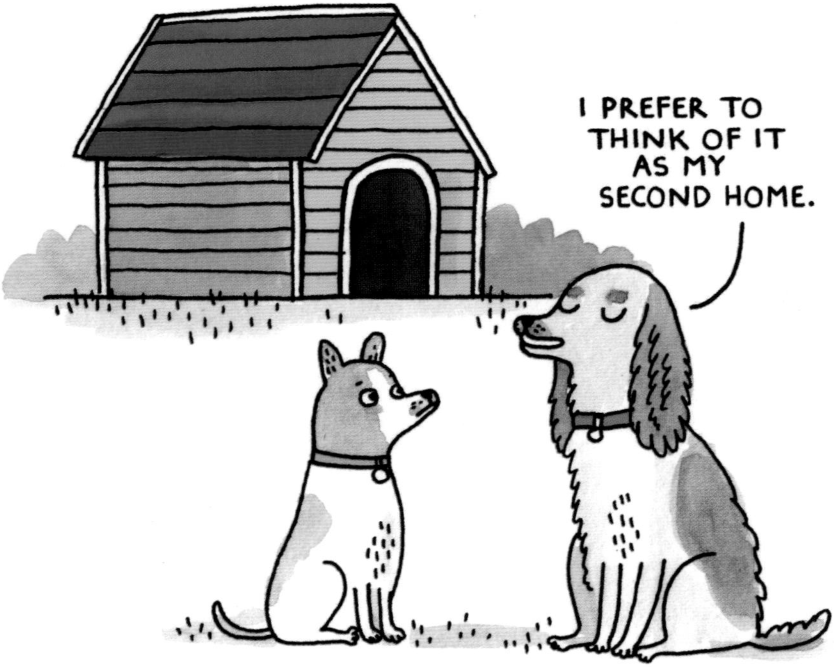
I PREFER TO THINK OF IT AS MY SECOND HOME.

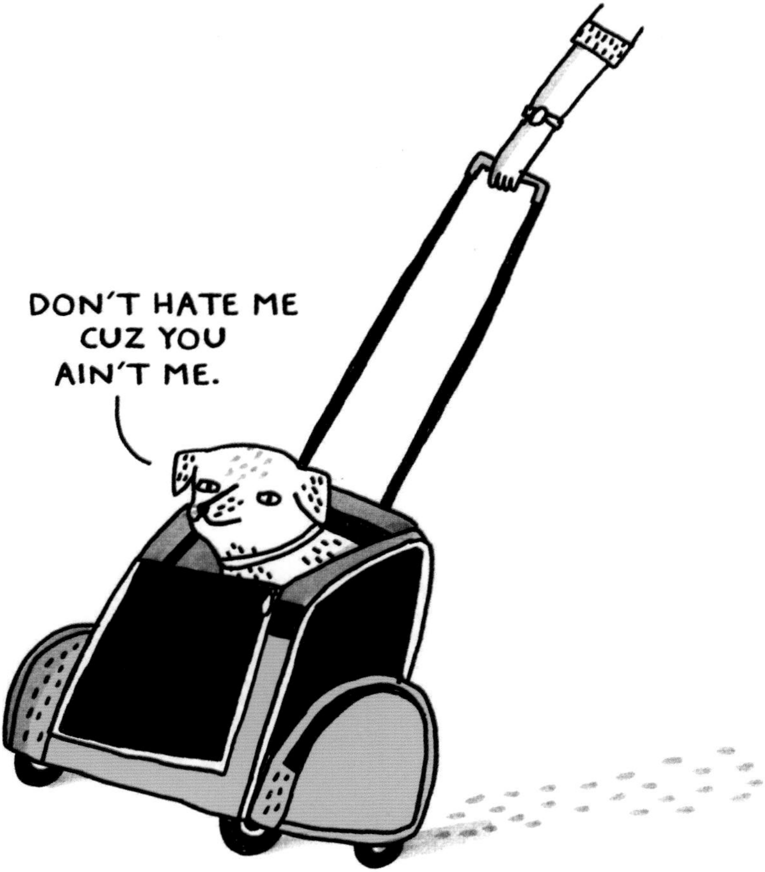
DON'T HATE ME
CUZ YOU
AIN'T ME.

AT THE DOGGIE
HOUSE OF HORRORS ...

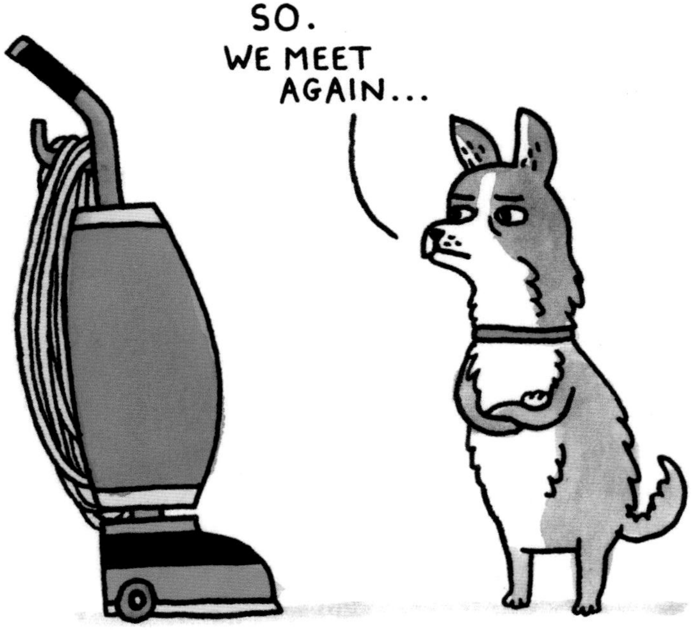
SO.
WE MEET
AGAIN...

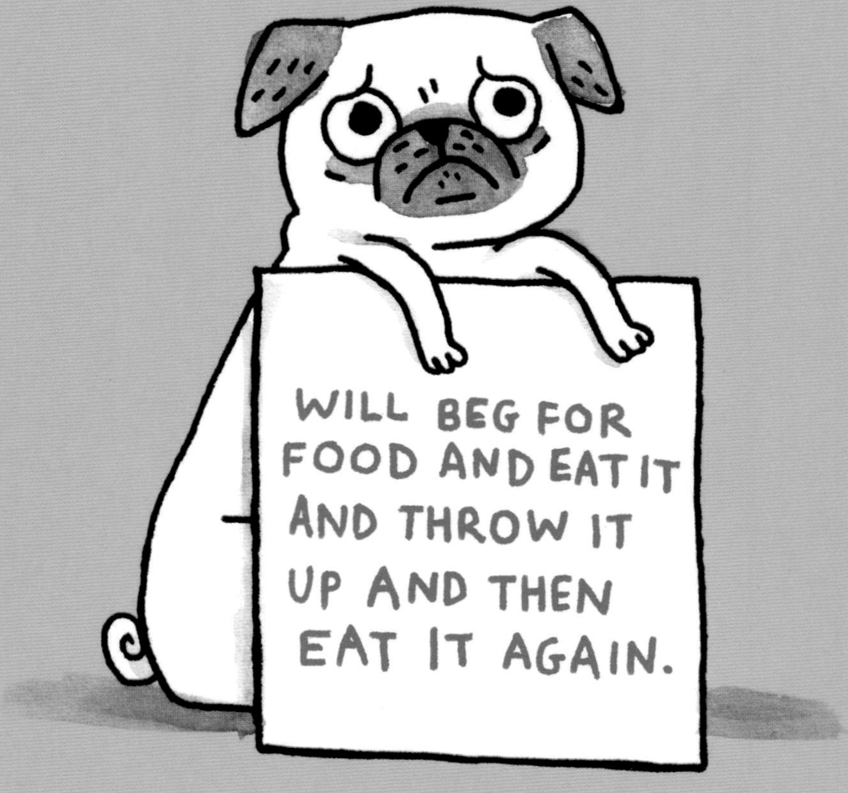
WILL BEG FOR FOOD AND EAT IT AND THROW IT UP AND THEN EAT IT AGAIN.

I MAY HAVE
INFORMATION
PERTAINING TO THE
WHEREABOUTS OF THE
MISSING HAM ...

DON'T
JUDGE
ME.

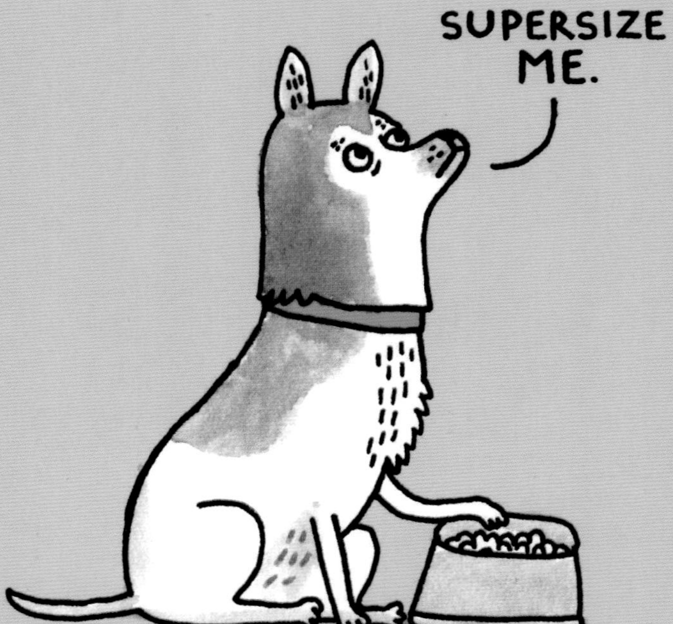
SUPERSIZE ME.

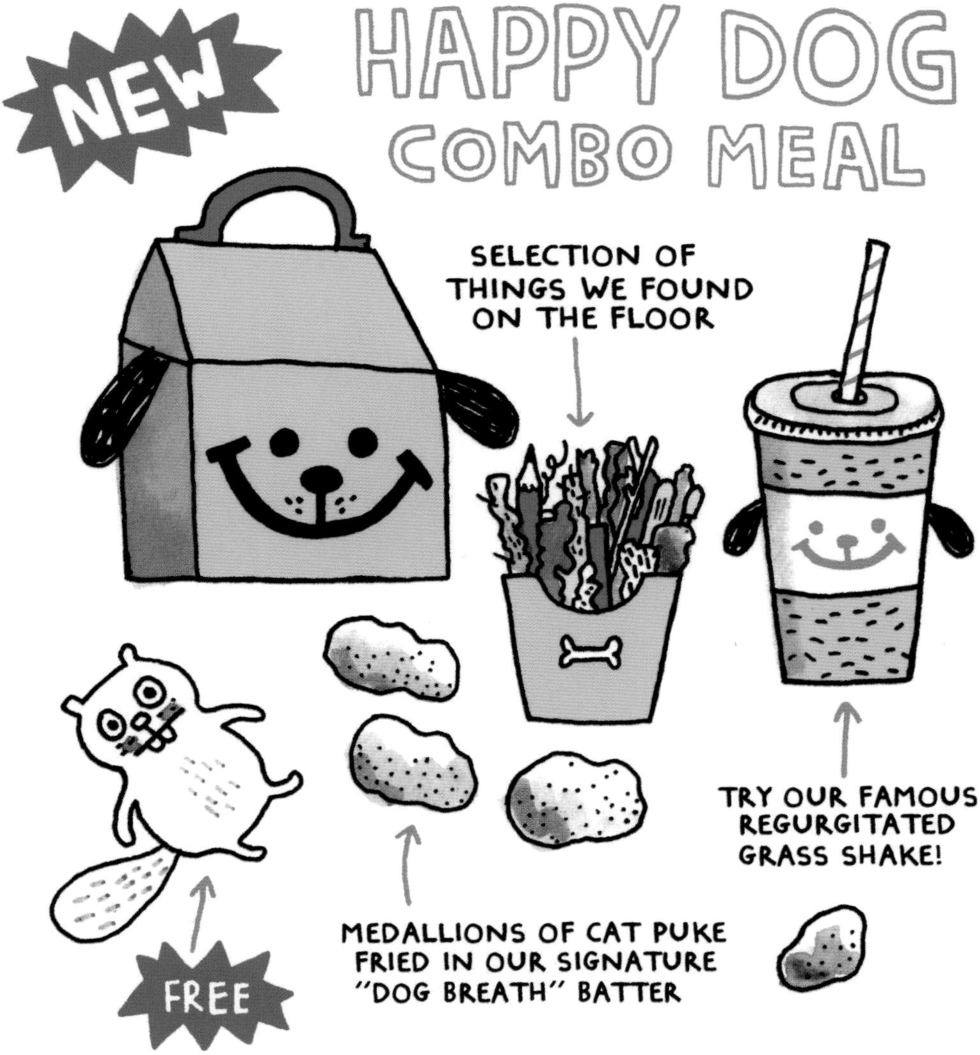
NEW
HAPPY DOG COMBO MEAL
SELECTION OF THINGS WE FOUND ON THE FLOOR
TRY OUR FAMOUS REGURGITATED GRASS SHAKE!
MEDALLIONS OF CAT PUKE FRIED IN OUR SIGNATURE "DOG BREATH" BATTER
FREE

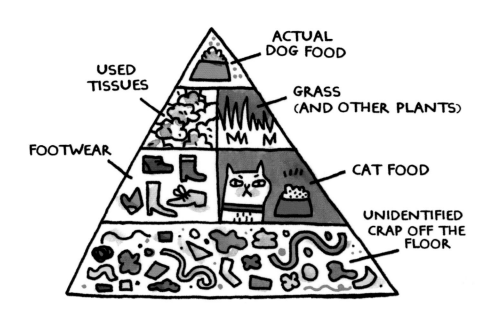

ACTUAL
DOG FOOD

USED
TISSUES

GRASS
(AND OTHER PLANTS)

FOOTWEAR

CAT FOOD

UNIDENTIFIED
CRAP OFF THE
FLOOR

DOGGIE FOOD PYRAMID

THE CAT THAT
GOT THE CREAM

Sigh.

THE DOG THAT
GOT THE
PARTIALLY
HYDROGENATED
SOY—BASED DAIRY
SUBSTITUTE

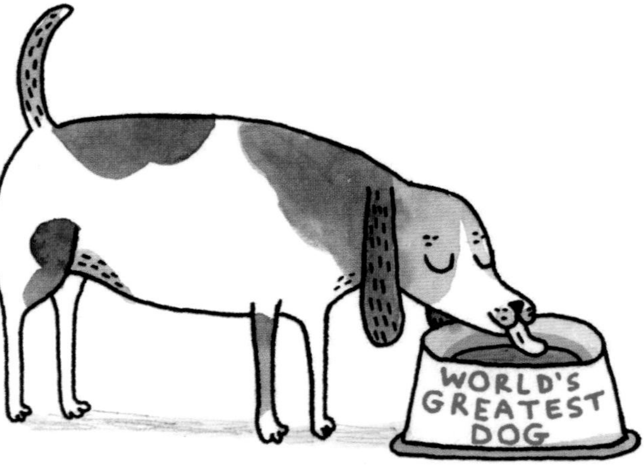
WORLD'S
GREATEST
DOG

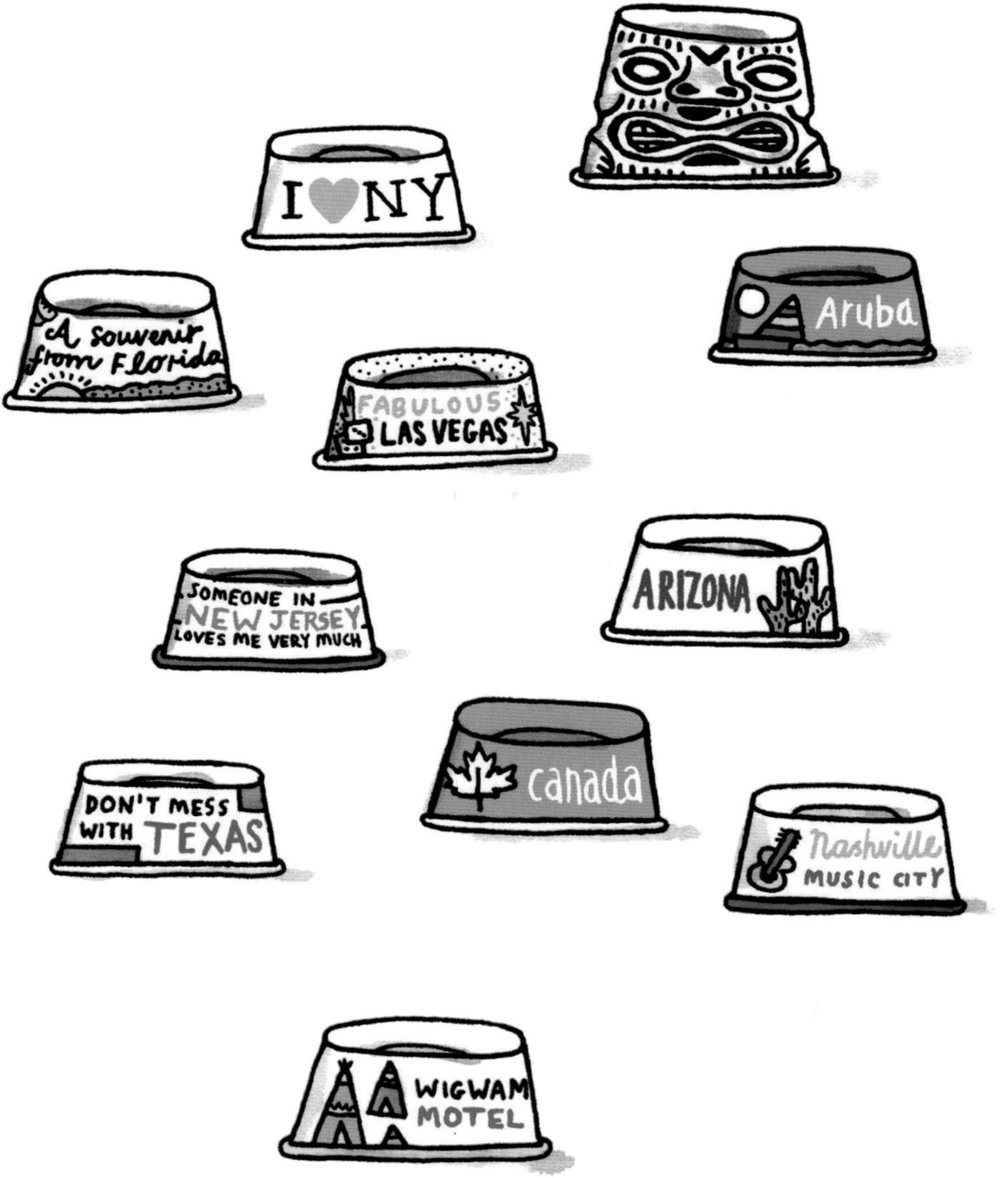
I ♥ NY
Aruba
A souvenir from Florida
FABULOUS LAS VEGAS
ARIZONA
SOMEONE IN NEW JERSEY LOVES ME VERY MUCH
canada
DON'T MESS WITH TEXAS
Nashville MUSIC CITY
WIGWAM MOTEL

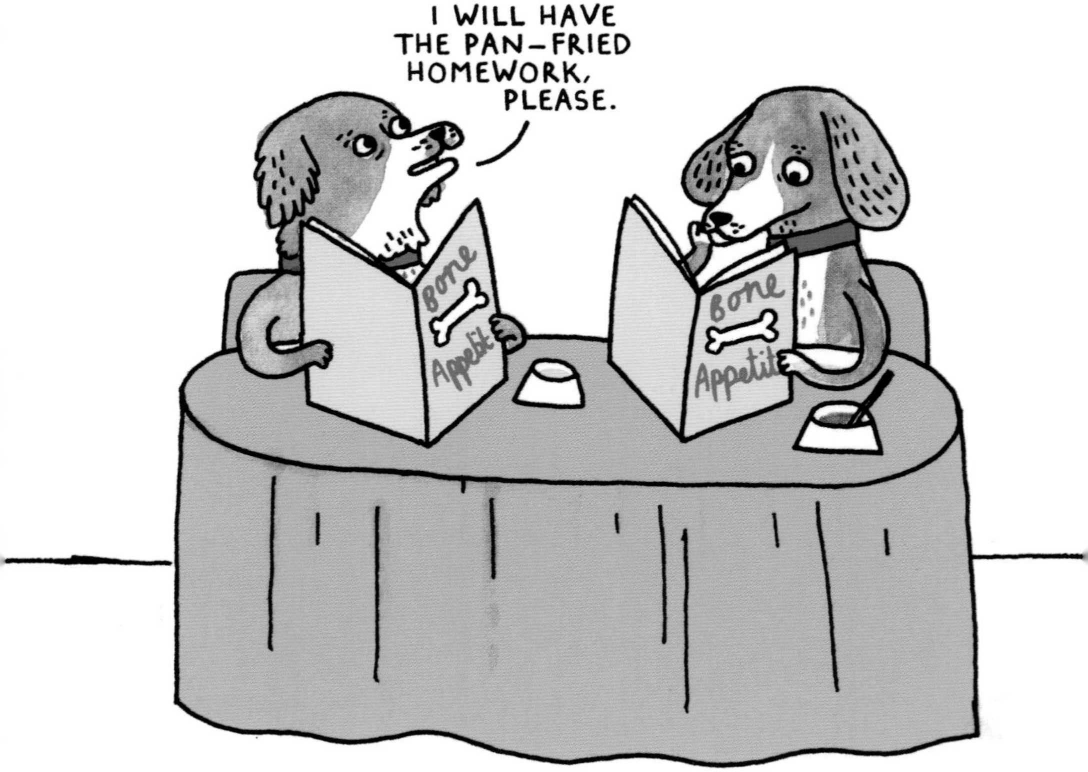
I WILL HAVE THE PAN-FRIED HOMEWORK, PLEASE.
Bone Appetit
Bone Appetit

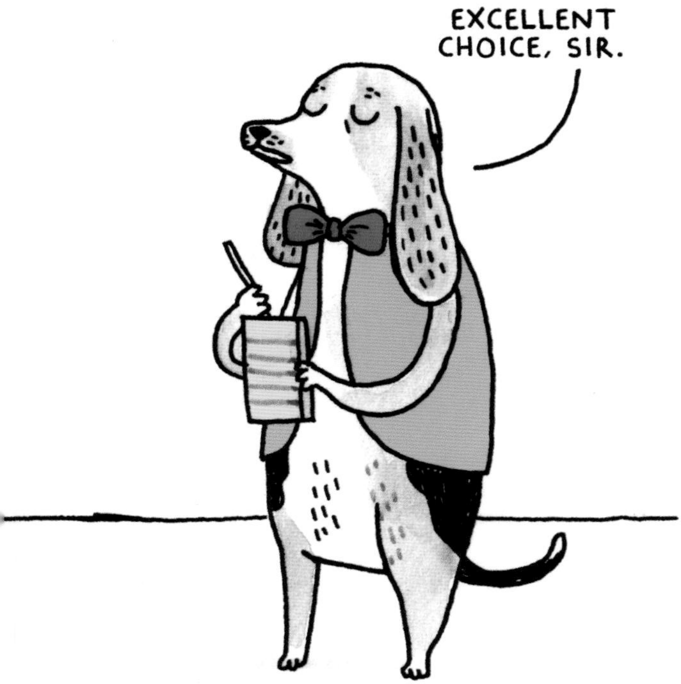
EXCELLENT
CHOICE, SIR.

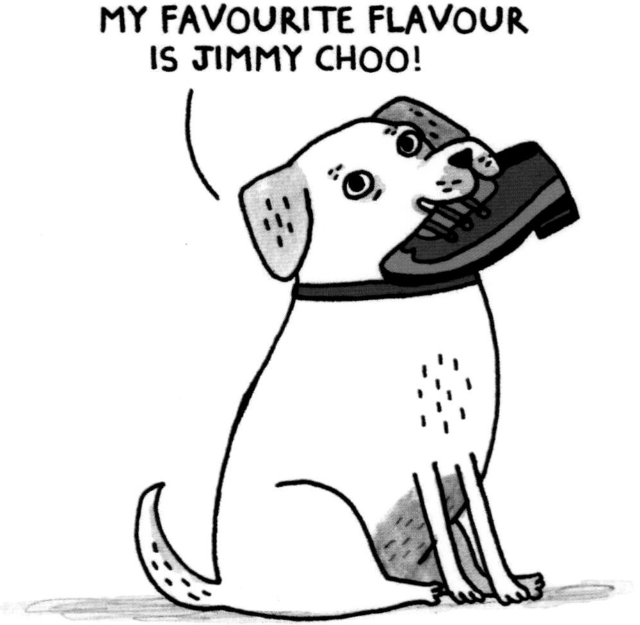
MY FAVOURITE FLAVOUR IS JIMMY CHOO!

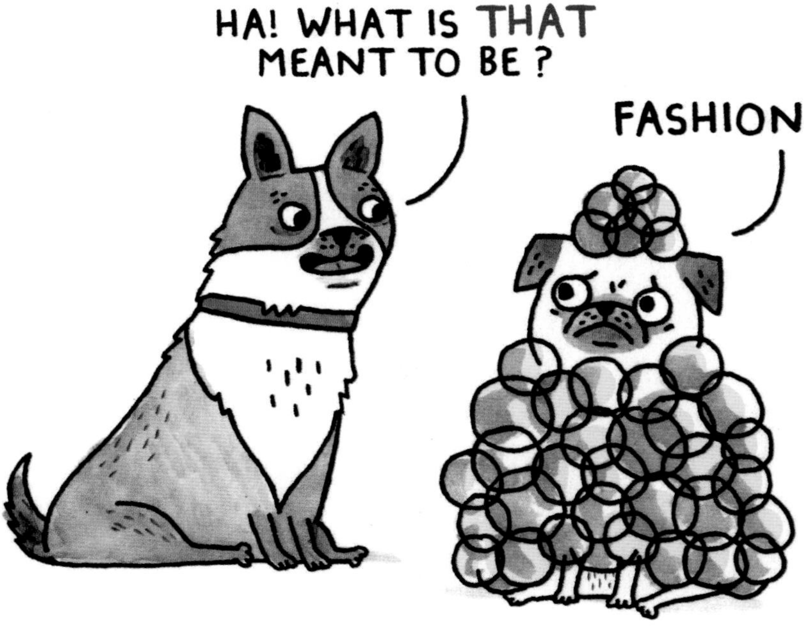
HA! WHAT IS THAT MEANT TO BE?
FASHION.

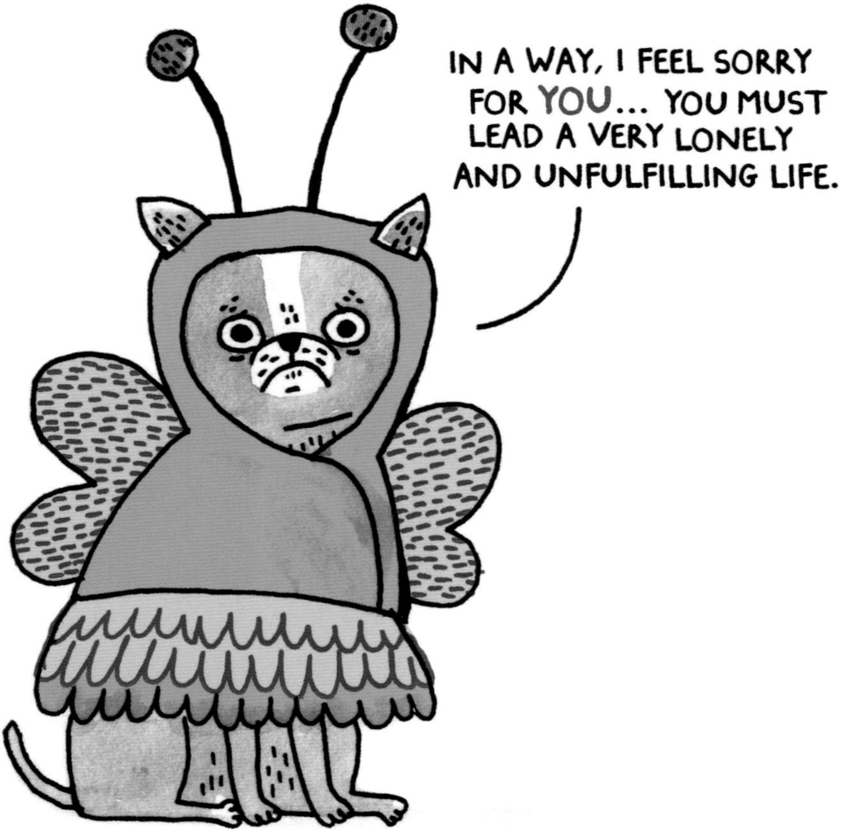
IN A WAY, I FEEL SORRY FOR YOU... YOU MUST LEAD A VERY LONELY AND UNFULFILLING LIFE.

# NEW DALMATION TRENDS

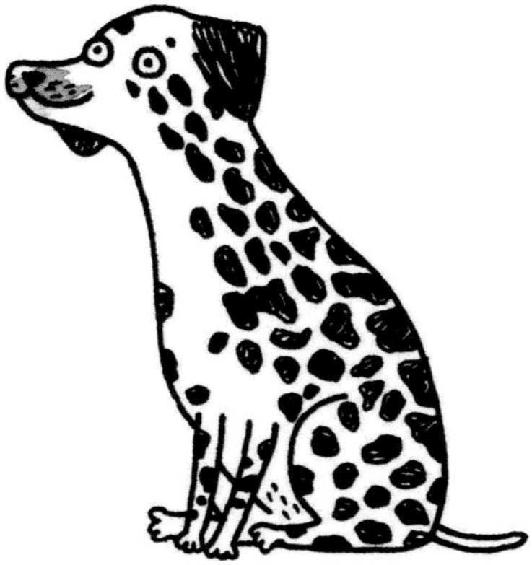

CLASSIC

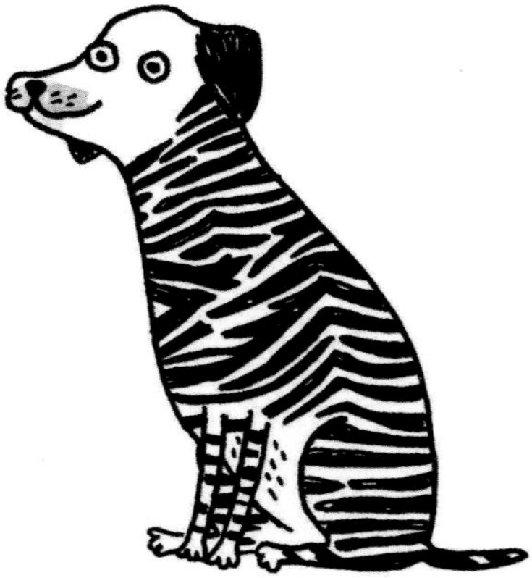

ZEBRA

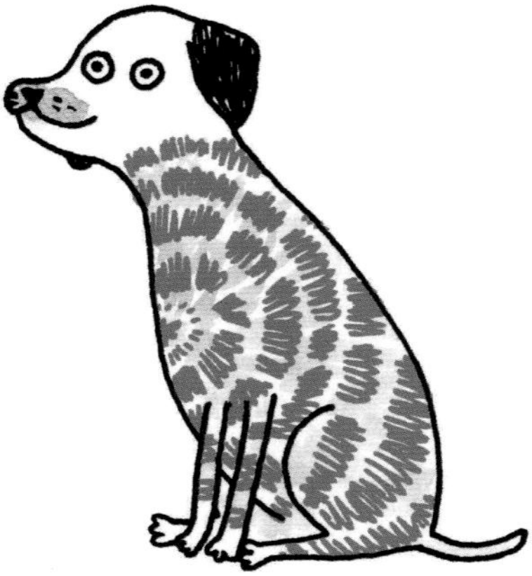

TIE-DYE

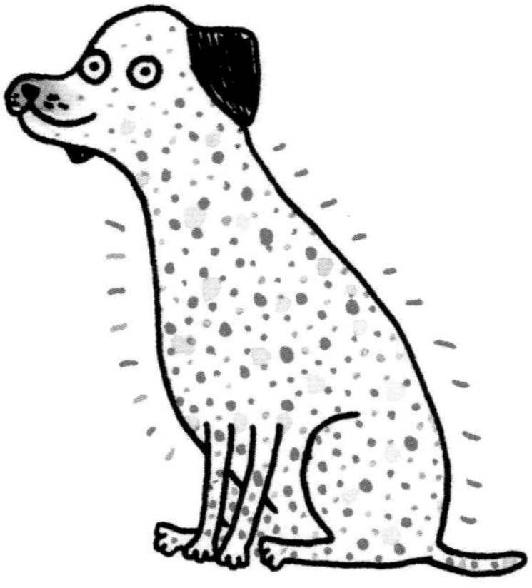

GLITTER

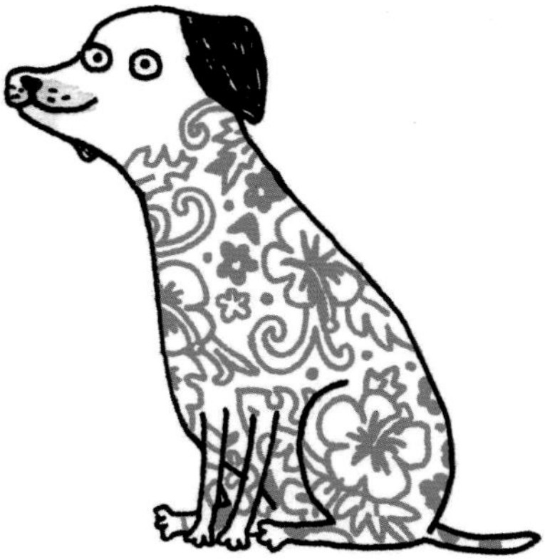

HAWAIIAN

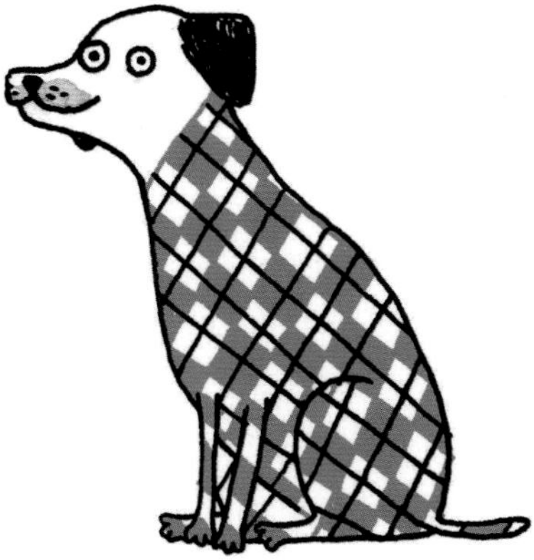

ARGYLE

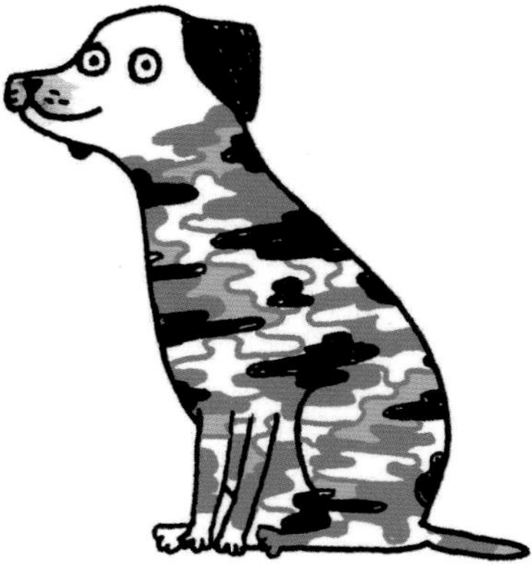

CAMO

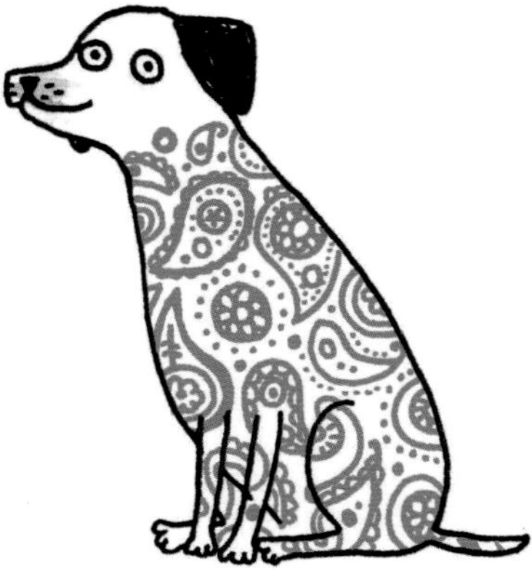

PAISLEY

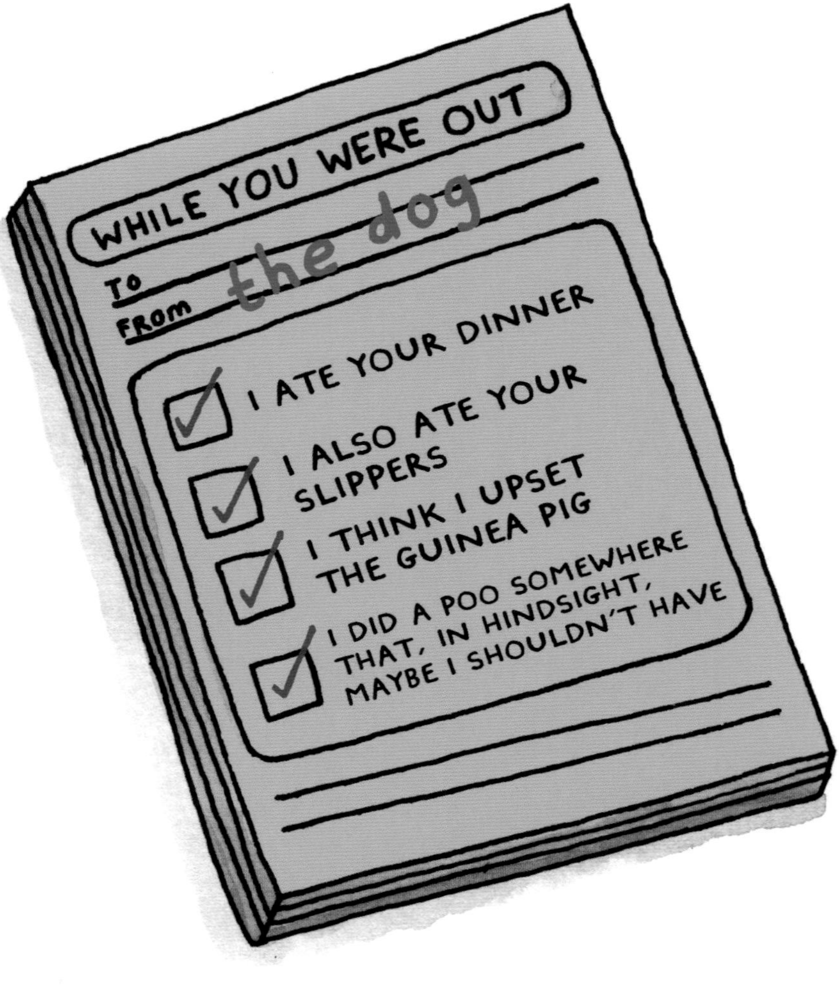
WHILE YOU WERE OUT
TO
FROM
the dog
I ATE YOUR DINNER
I ALSO ATE YOUR SLIPPERS
I THINK I UPSET THE GUINEA PIG
I DID A POO SOMEWHERE THAT, IN HINDSIGHT, MAYBE I SHOULDN'T HAVE

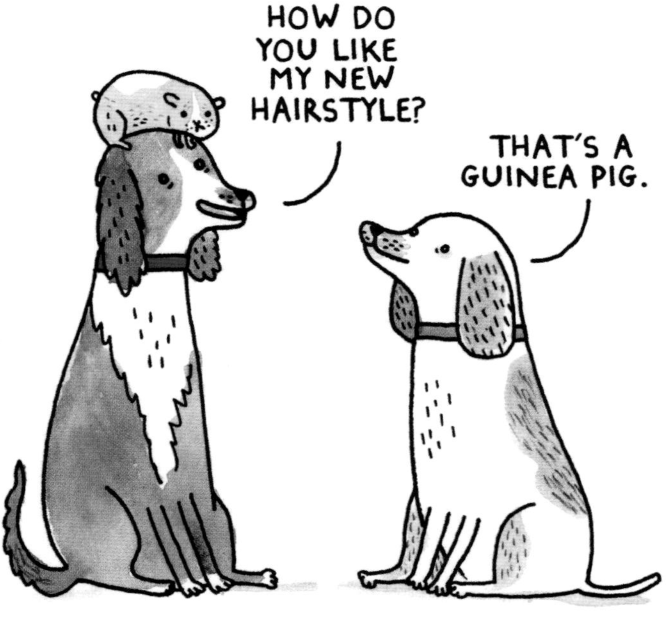
HOW DO YOU LIKE MY NEW HAIRSTYLE?
THAT'S A GUINEA PIG.

# SOME HIGHLIGHTS FROM THIS YEAR'S
## *SALONE INTERNAZIONALE DEI DOG BEDS DI MILANO*

**THE LAUNDRY BASKET**
BY LUIGI DI LAVANDERIA

**THE SUNBED**
BY GIULIA D'ABBRONZATURA

**THE BASSINET 'O' BACON**
BY MARIO PANCETTA

**THE THROWING HAND CHAIR**
BY VALENTINA DEL TENNIS BALL

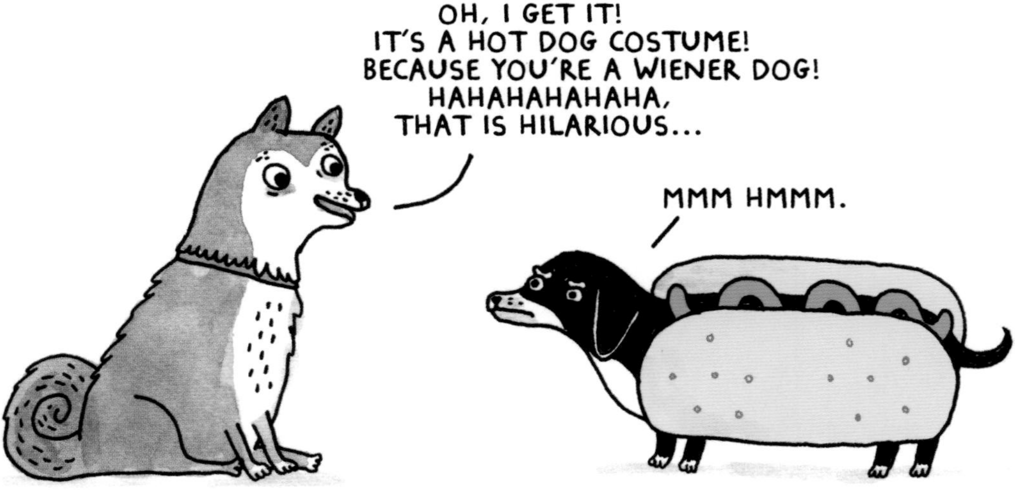
OH, I GET IT!
IT'S A HOT DOG COSTUME!
BECAUSE YOU'RE A WIENER DOG!
HAHAHAHAHAHA,
THAT IS HILARIOUS...
MMM HMMM.

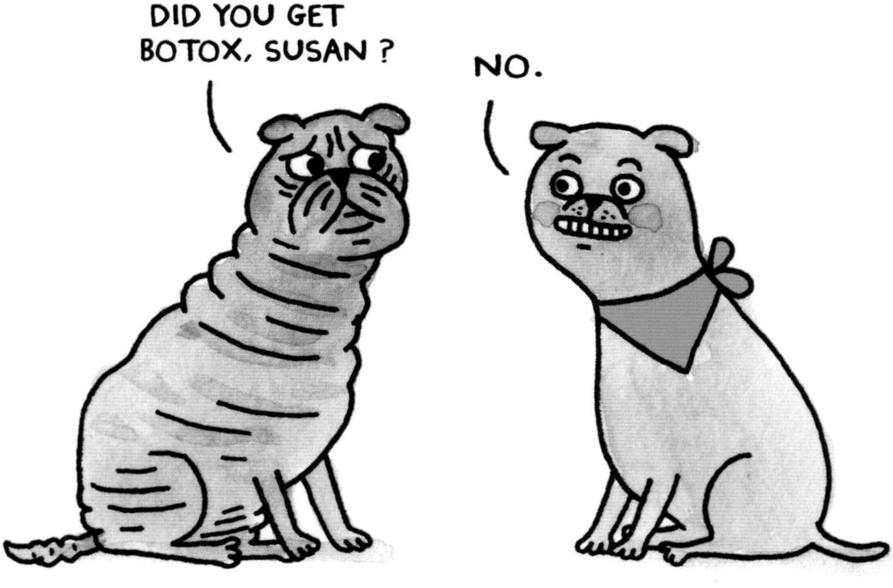
DID YOU GET BOTOX, SUSAN ?
NO.

# DOGS IN BONNETS

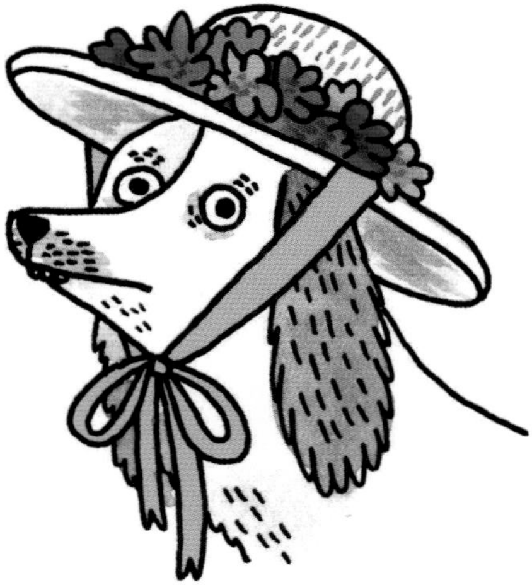

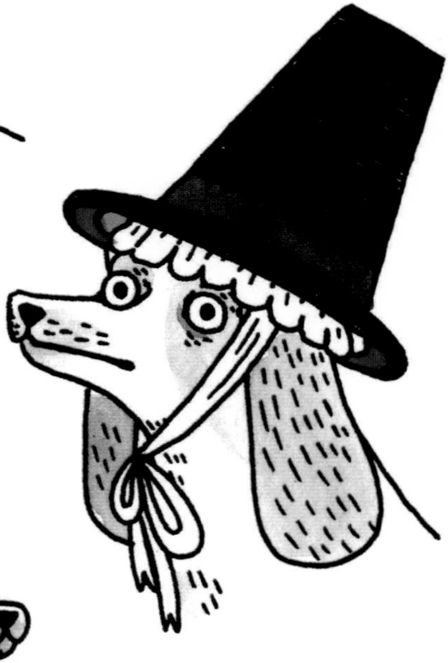

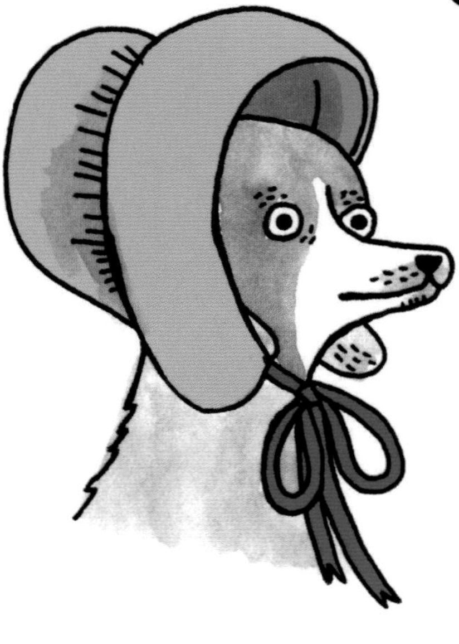

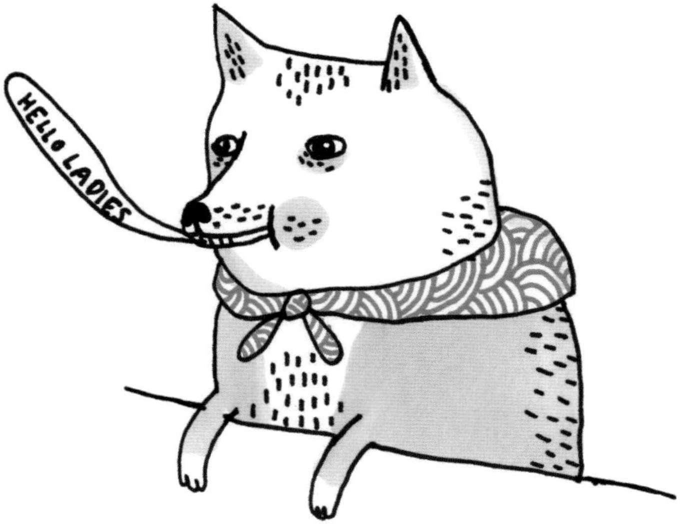
HELLO LADIES

GRAHAM KNEW THAT HIS PENCHANT FOR WEARING JAUNTY SCARVES MADE HIM SOMETHING OF A LOCAL HEART THROB.

# ESSENTIAL OILS

ESSENCE OF BUTTS

ORGANIC CAT PISS

MILK OF TENNIS BALLS

OIL OF SQUIRREL

PEANUT BUTTER ROOT

PURE PUDDLE WATER

ESSENCE OF SOCK

GRAVY BONE BALM

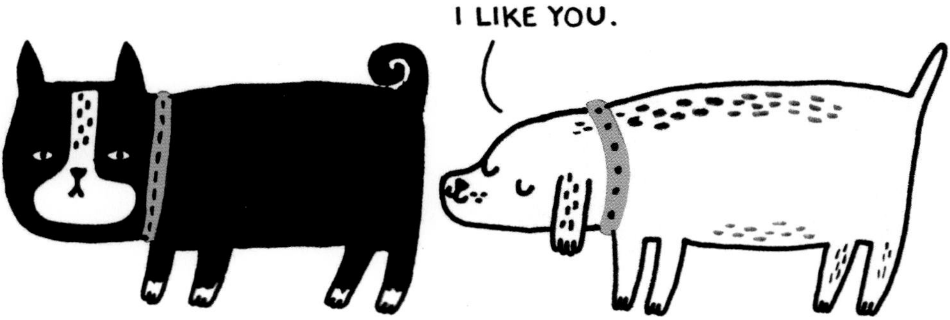
I LIKE YOU.

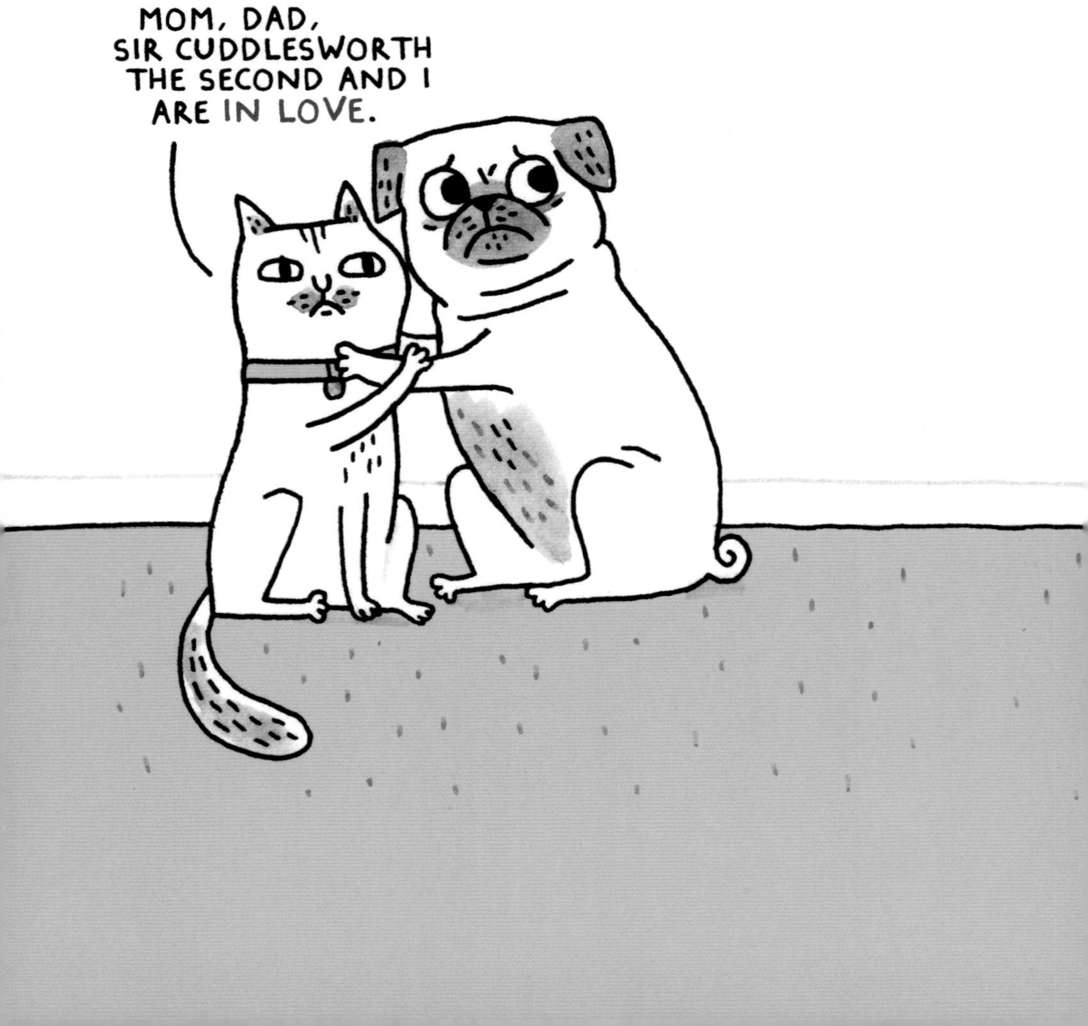
MOM, DAD, SIR CUDDLESWORTH THE SECOND AND I ARE IN LOVE.

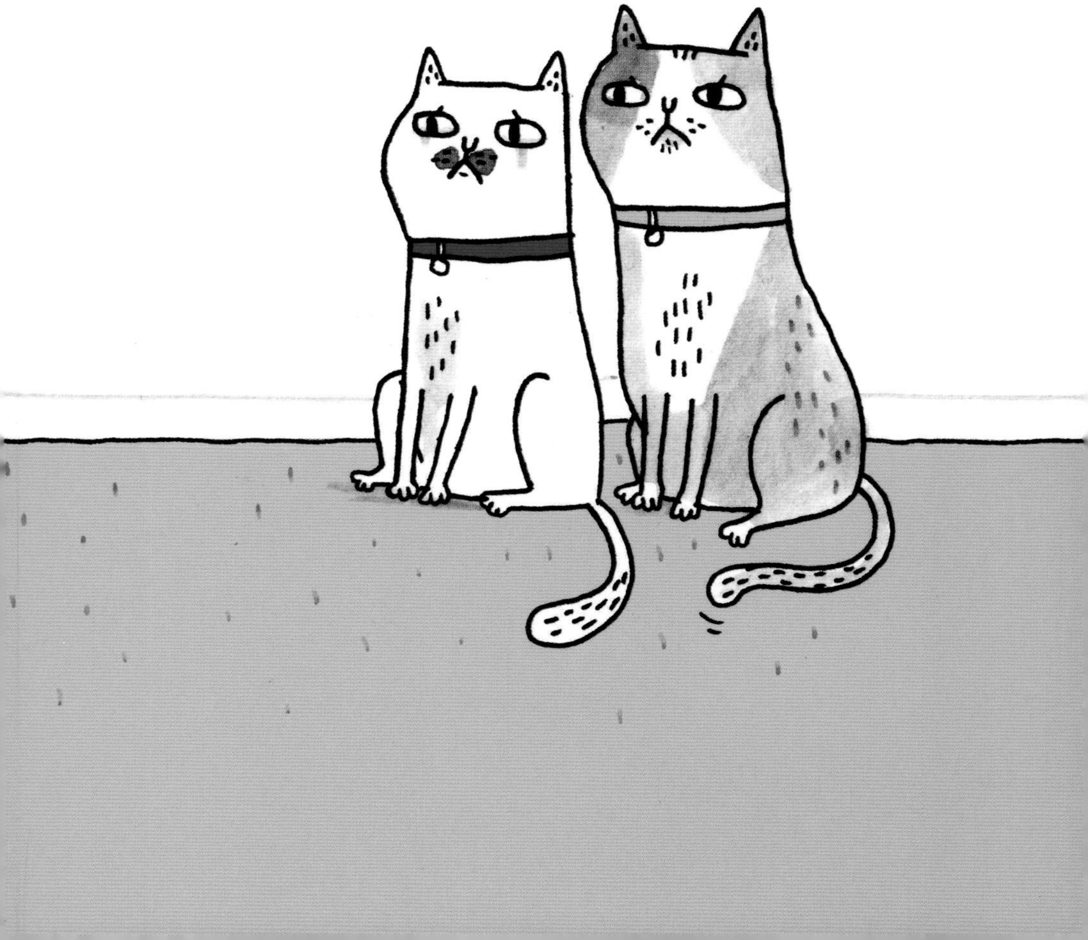

HEY! WHAT'S GOING ON? WANT TO HANG OUT? LET'S GO TO THE PARK! OOOH, AND CAN WE PLAY WITH A STICK? THAT WOULD BE **SO** COOL! YOU'RE THE BEST!

MAN'S BEST FRIEND

HEY, WHAT HAVE YOU GOT FOR ME? NOTHING? OK, SEE YOU LATER THEN, I GUESS.

MAN'S CASUAL ACQUAINTANCE

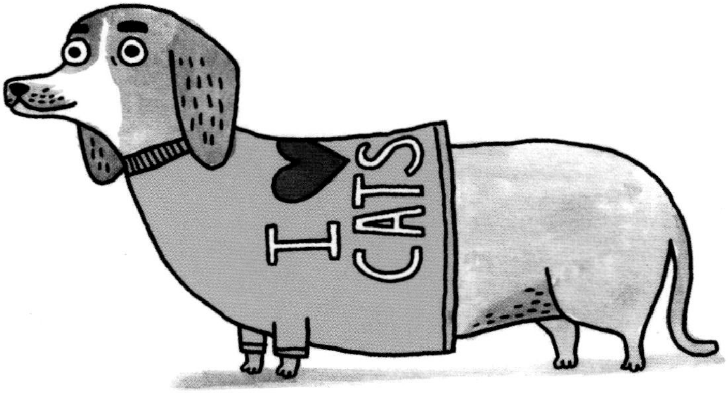
I ♥ CATS

DOG WEARING AN "IRONIC" T-SHIRT

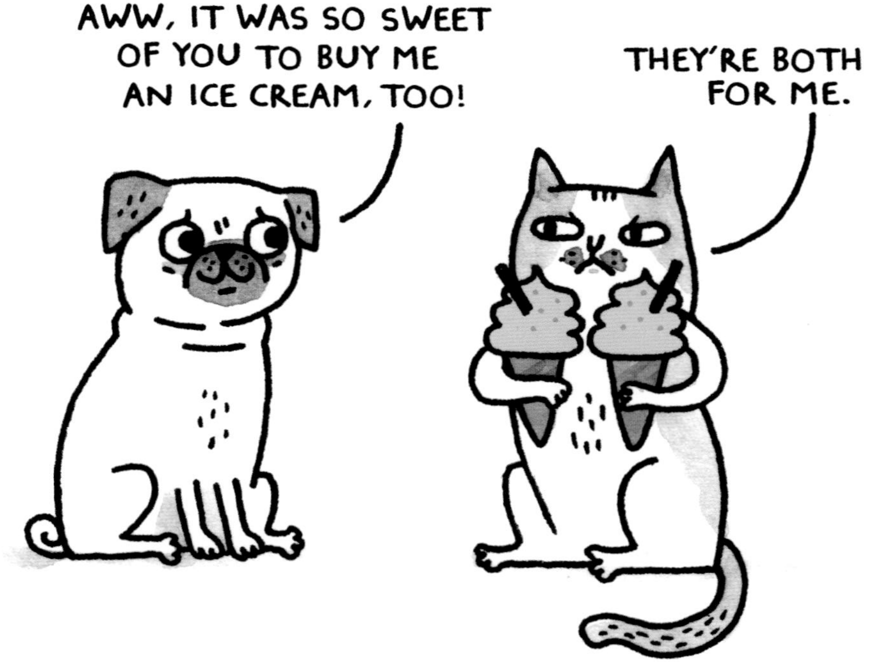
AWW, IT WAS SO SWEET OF YOU TO BUY ME AN ICE CREAM, TOO!
THEY'RE BOTH FOR ME.

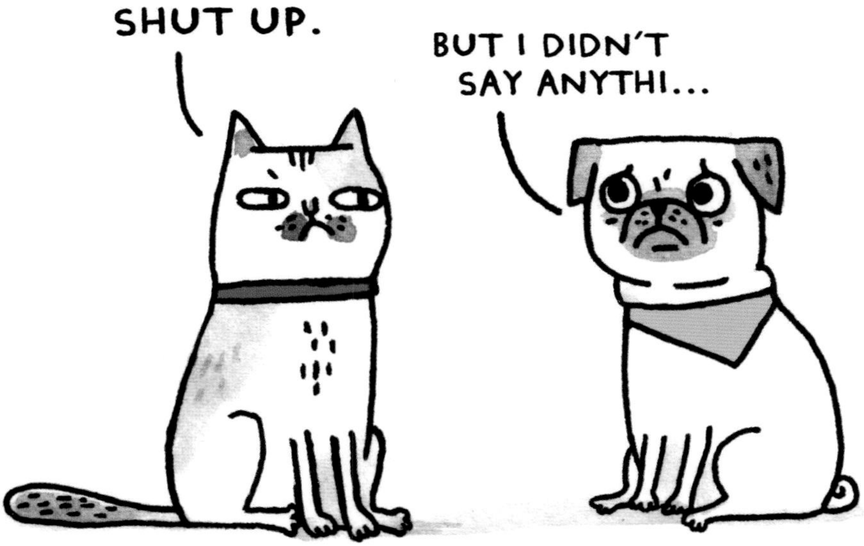
SHUT UP.
BUT I DIDN'T SAY ANYTHI...

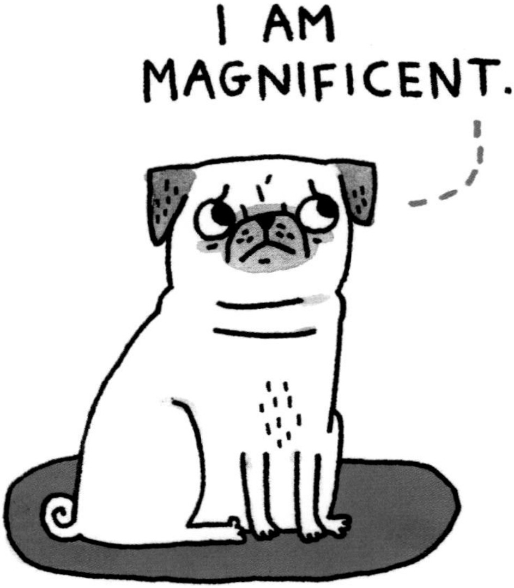
I AM
MAGNIFICENT.

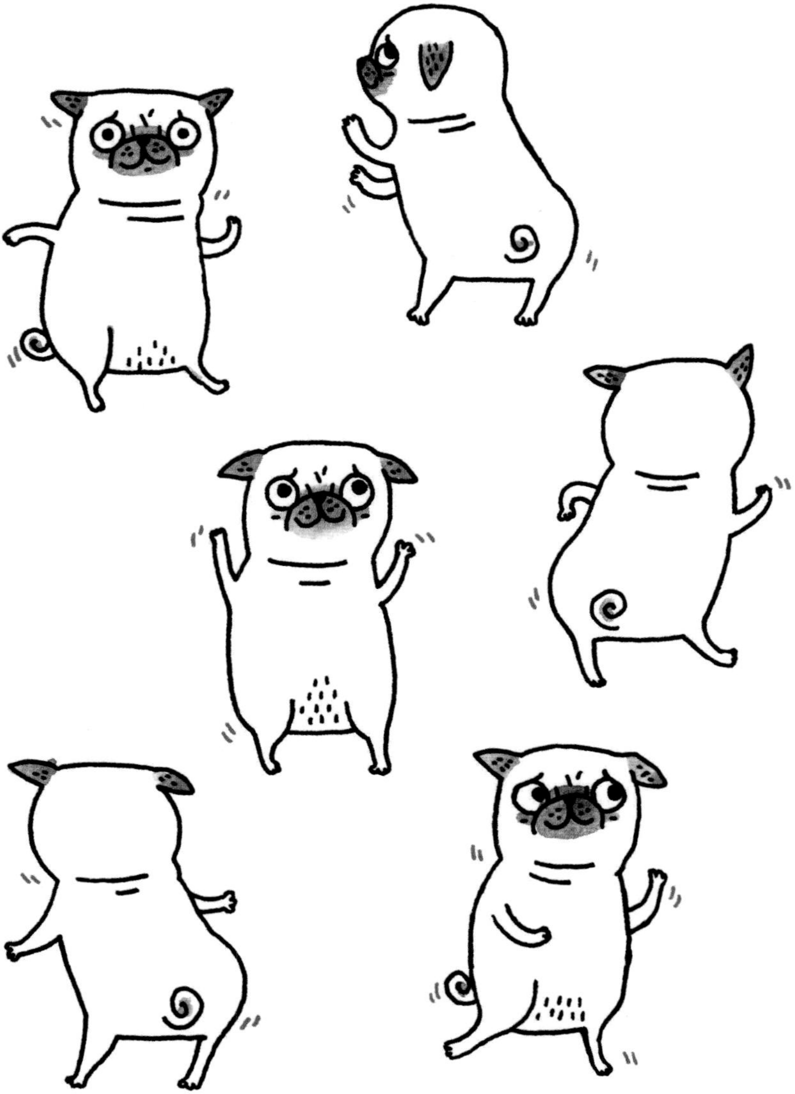

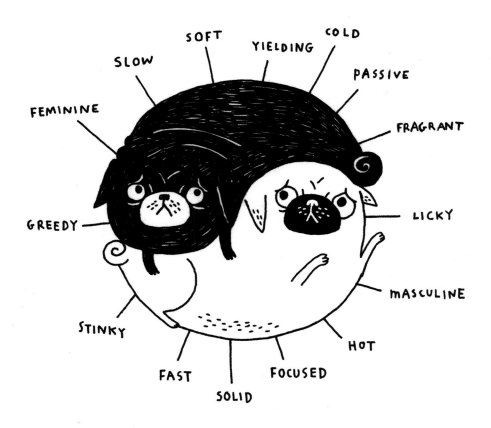

SLOW SOFT YIELDING COLD

PASSIVE

FEMININE

FRAGRANT

GREEDY

LICKY

MASCULINE

STINKY

HOT

FAST FOCUSED

SOLID

The TAO OF PUG

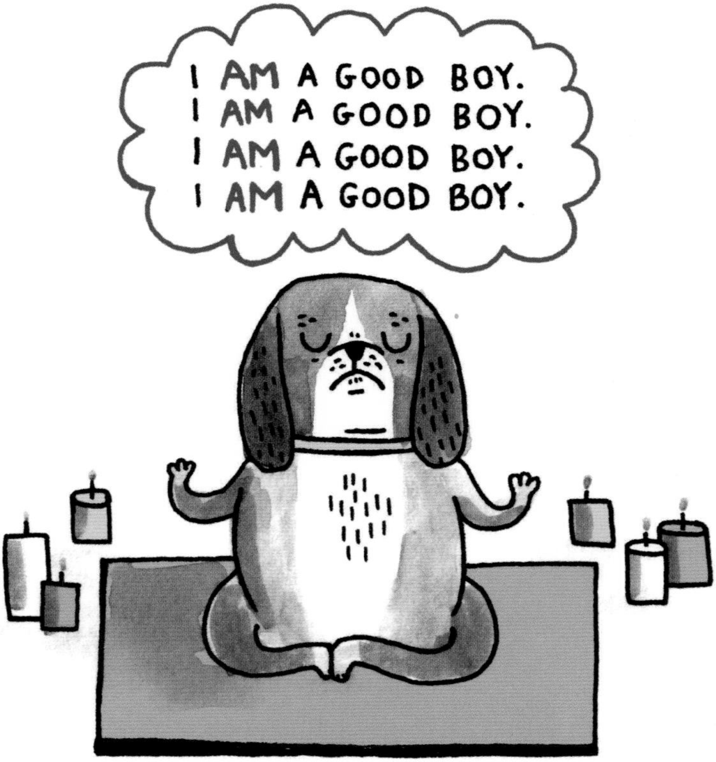
I AM A GOOD BOY.
I AM A GOOD BOY.
I AM A GOOD BOY.
I AM A GOOD BOY.

EVERY DAY BEFORE DINNER,
BRIAN PRACTICES HIS
POSITIVE AFFIRMATIONS.

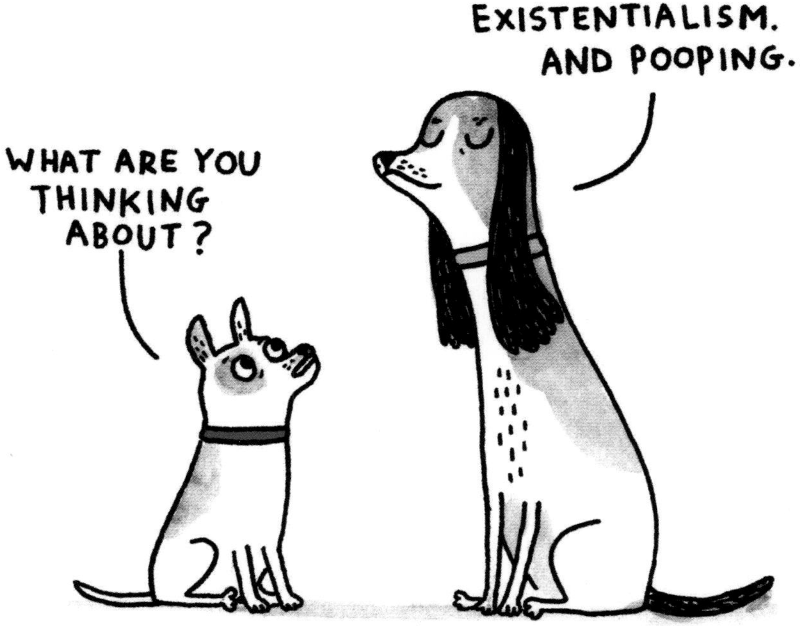
WHAT ARE YOU THINKING ABOUT?
EXISTENTIALISM. AND POOPING.

## CANINE LITERATURE

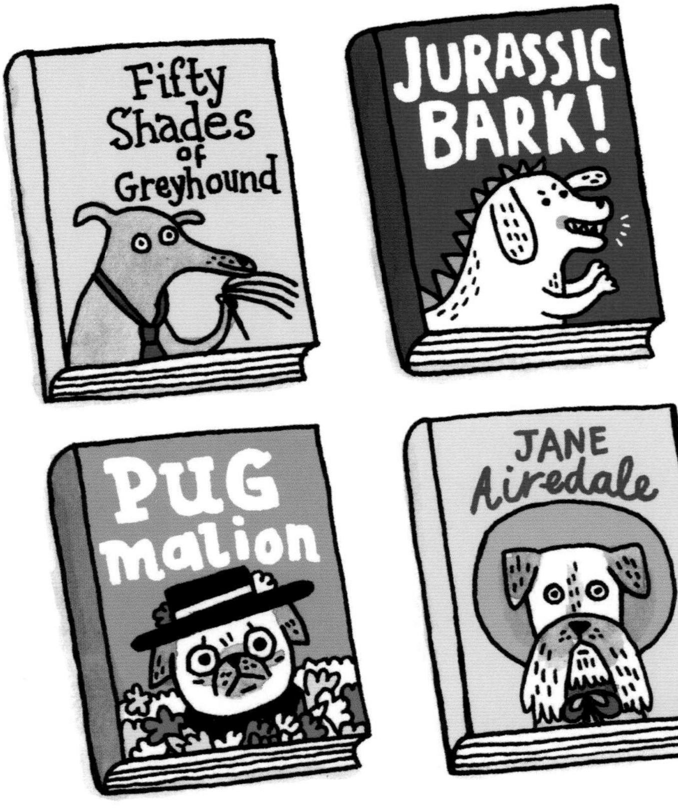
Fifty Shades of Greyhound
JURASSIC BARK!
PUG malion
JANE Airedale

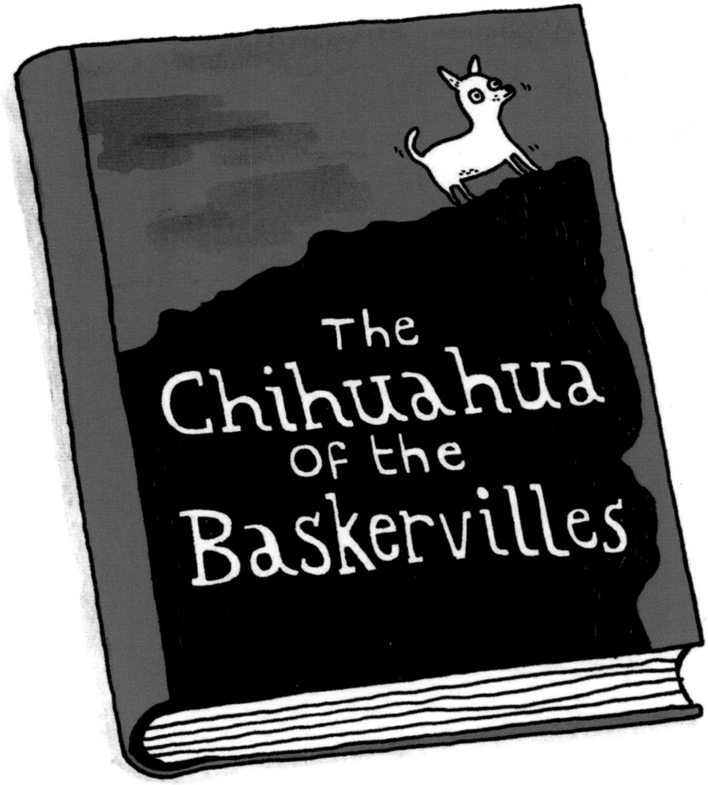
The
Chihuahua
of the
Baskervilles

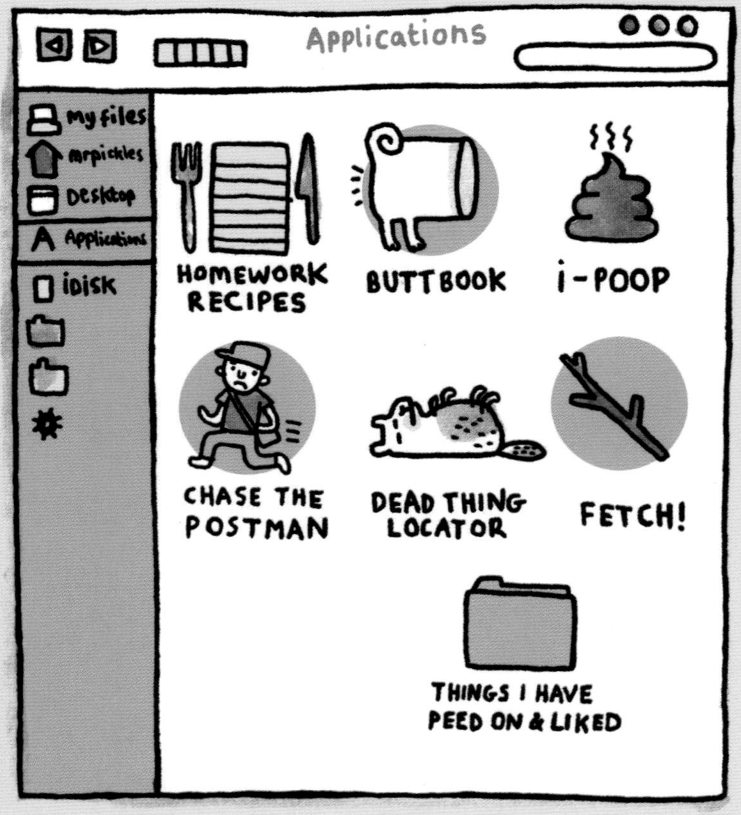

Applications
my files
mrpickles
Desktop
Applications
idisk
HOMEWORK RECIPES
BUTTBOOK
i-POOP
CHASE THE POSTMAN
DEAD THING LOCATOR
FETCH!
THINGS I HAVE PEED ON & LIKED

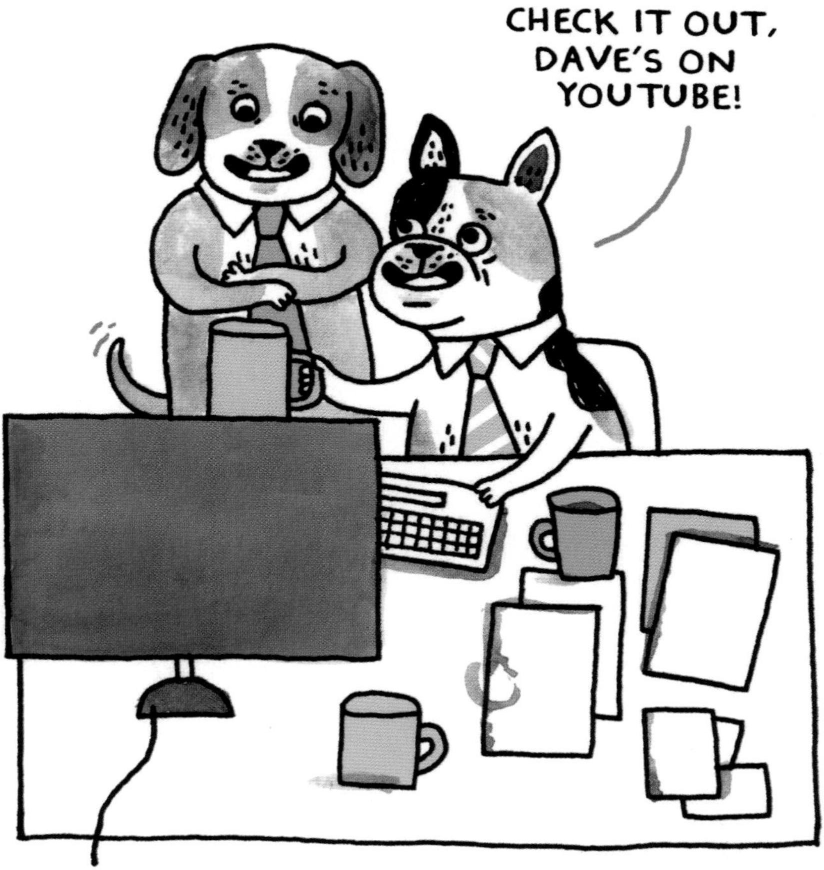
CHECK IT OUT, DAVE'S ON YOUTUBE!

"WORKING" DOGS

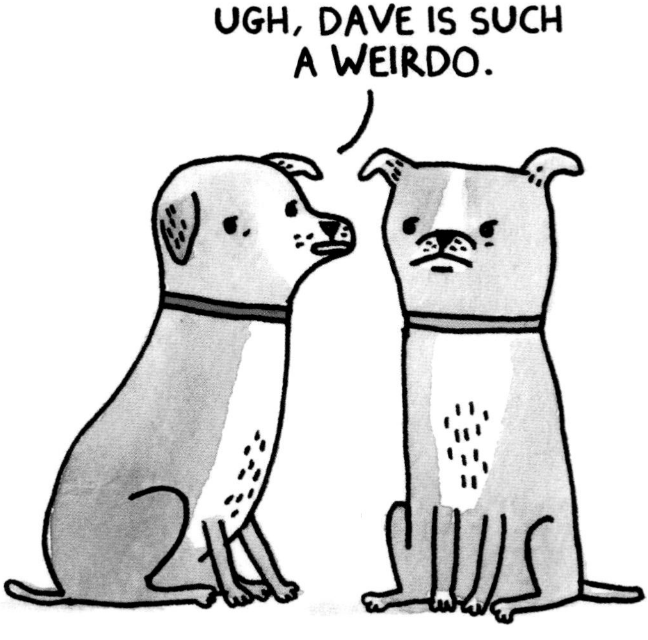
UGH, DAVE IS SUCH A WEIRDO.

PLEASE GOD,
DON'T LET ME BUMP
INTO THE GUYS
LOOKING LIKE THIS.

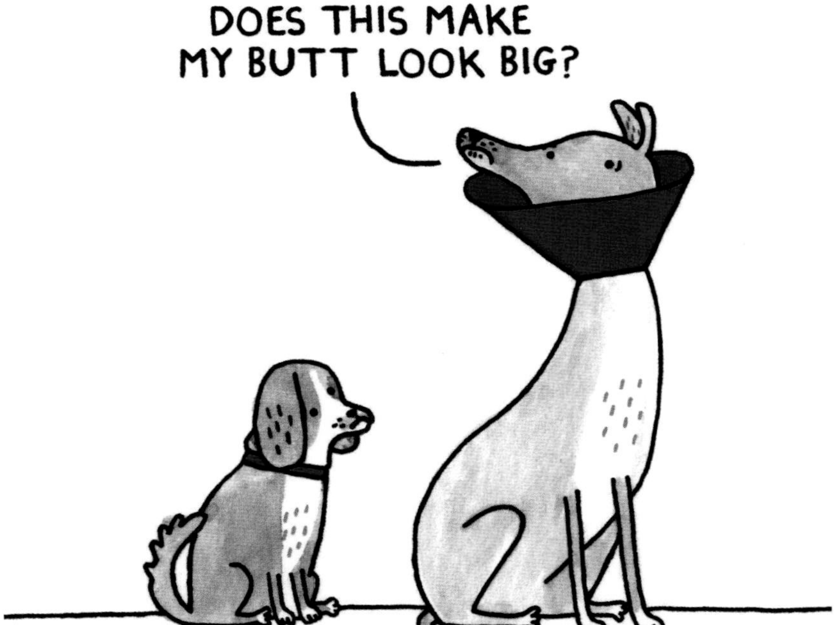
DOES THIS MAKE
MY BUTT LOOK BIG?

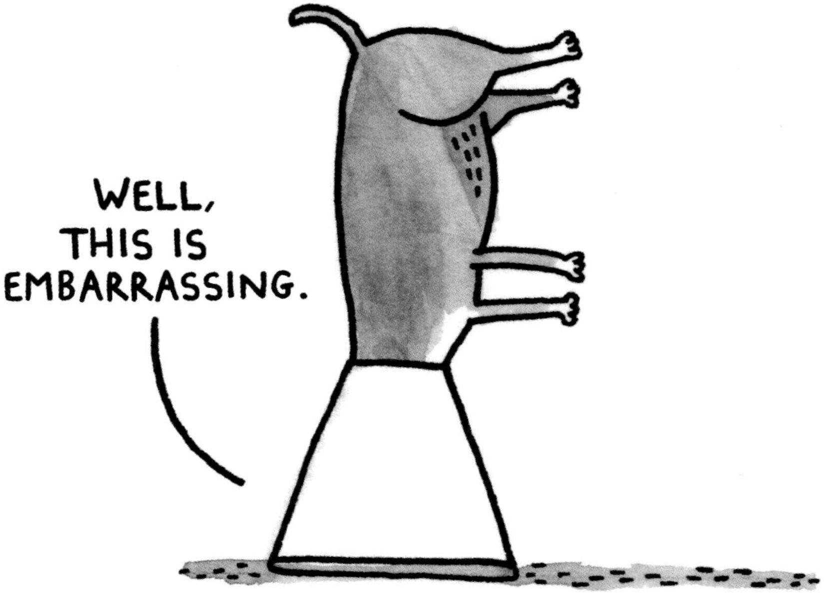
WELL,
THIS IS
EMBARRASSING.

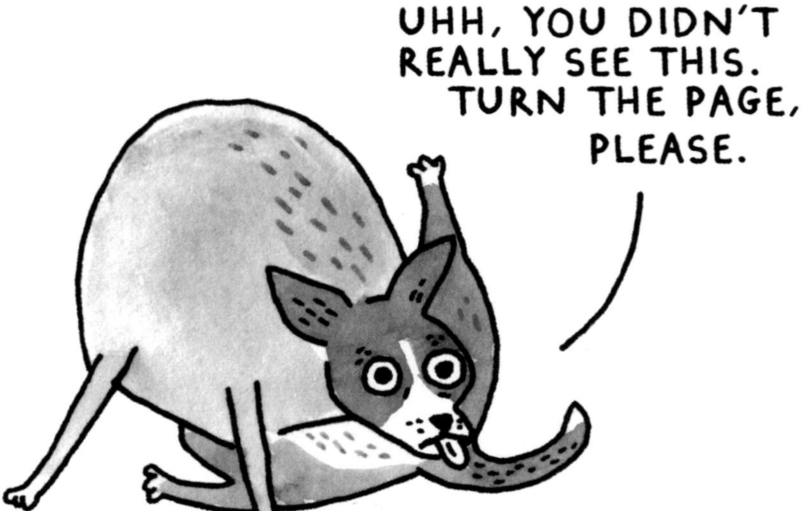
UHH, YOU DIDN'T REALLY SEE THIS. TURN THE PAGE, PLEASE.

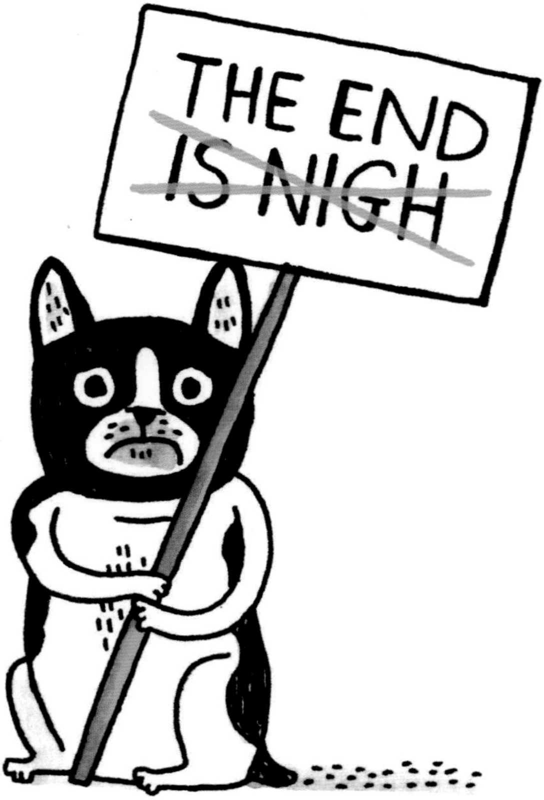
THE END
IS NIGH

**Gemma Correll** has qualifications in basic first aid, grade 5 flute, as well as a first-class degree in Graphic Design and Illustration from the Norwich School of Art and Design (U.K.). These skills have enabled her to forge a career in freelance illustration and cartooning (and also help you out if you break your finger). Gemma's work is narrative-based with a strong emphasis on word play, humor, observational journalism, and cats. She divides her time between commissioned work, producing illustrations for clients including *The New York Times* and Hallmark, and working on personal projects, such as designing and selling her own range of products. She has exhibited around the world in Asia, Canada, the United States, and Europe. Gemma currently lives in Norwich, England, where she devotes a large proportion of her time to drinking coffee, rummaging in junk shops, and attending to the whims of her pugs, Mr. Pickles and Bella.

**Gemma Correll** hat Qualifikationen in Erster Hilfe, sie spielt Flöte mit Schwierigkeitsgrad 5 und sie hat einen erstklassigen Abschluss in Graphikdesign und Illustration von der Norwich School of Art and Design (UK). Durch diese Fertigkeiten konnte sie sich als freiberufliche Illustratorin und Cartoon-Zeichnerin einen Namen machen (und sie kann Ihnen helfen, falls Sie sich einen Finger brechen). Gemmas Arbeit basiert auf Erzählungen, bei denen Wortspiele, Humor, beobachtender Journalismus und Katzen im Mittelpunkt stehen. Sie teilt ihre Zeit zwischen Auftragsarbeiten, Illustrationen für Kunden wie *The New York Times* und Hallmark auf und sie arbeitet an ihren persönlichen Projekten, wie dem Design und Verkauf ihrer eigenen Produktpalette. Sie hat in aller Welt in Asien, Kanada, den USA und Europa ausgestellt. Derzeit lebt Gemma im englischen Norwich, wo sie einen Großteil ihrer Zeit mit Kaffee trinken, dem Herumsuchen in Trödelläden und damit verbringt, den Launen ihrer Möpse Mr. Pickles und Bella nachzugeben.

**Gemma Correll** a des qualifications en secourisme élémentaire, un cinquième niveau de flute, ainsi qu'un diplôme de première classe en graphisme et illustration de l'École des Arts de Norwich (Royaume-Uni). Ces talents lui ont permis de faire carrière en freelance dans le dessin et les bandes dessinées (et aussi de vous venir en aide si vous vous cassez le doigt). L'œuvre de Gemma est un récit où règnent les jeux de mots, l'humour, le journalisme d'immersion et les chats. Elle partage son temps entre le travail à la commande, la production d'illustrations pour ses clients comme *The New York Times* et Hallmark et ses projets personnels comme le dessin et la vente de sa propre gamme de produits. Elle a fait des expositions dans le monde entier, en Asie, au Canada, aux États-Unis et en Europe. Gemma vit à présent à Norwich, Angleterre où elle consacre une large partie de son temps à boire du café, farfouiller dans les boutiques de bric à brac et satisfaire les moindres caprices de ses carlins, Mr. Pickles et Bella.

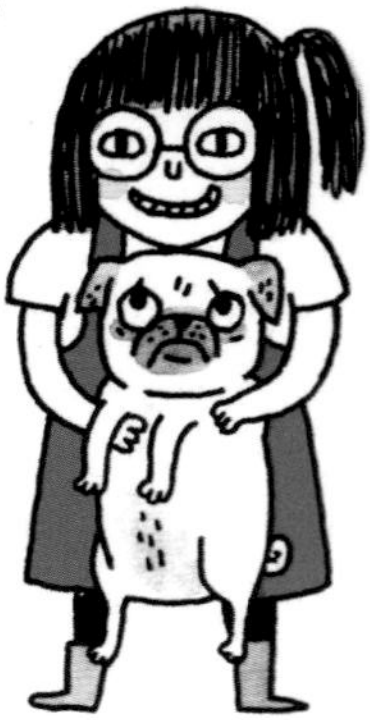

**Seamus Mullarkey** is a New York-based writer who thinks dogs have made it. Samples of his work can be perused at seamusmullarkey.com.

**Seamus Mullarkey** ist ein in New York City ansässiger Schriftsteller, der meint, dass Hunde es geschafft haben. Beispiele seiner Arbeit befinden sich auf seamusmullarkey.com.

**Seamus Mullarkey** est un écrivain qui vit à New York et il pense que les chiens ont brillamment réussi. Vous pouvez parcourir des exemples de son œuvre sur seamusmullarkey.com.

*A Dog's Life*
Copyright © 2013 Gemma Correll. All rights reserved.

Picture and text rights reserved for all countries.
No part of this publication may be reproduced in any manner whatsoever.

Artwork: Gemma Correll
Editor: Anshana Arora
Design: Allison Stern
Introduction: Seamus Mullarkey
Translations: Carmen Berelson (German); Helena Solodky-Wang (French)

Published by teNeues Publishing Group

teNeues Verlag GmbH + Co. KG
Am Selder 37, 47906 Kempen, Germany
Phone: 0049-(0)2152-916-0
Fax: 0049-(0)2152-916-111
E-mail: books@teneues.de

Press Department:
arehn@teneues.de
Phone: 0049-(0)2152-916-202

teNeues Digital Media GmBH
Kohlfurter Strasse 41-43, 10999 Berlin, Germany
Phone: 0049-(0)30-60-031102
e-mail: mail@tndm.de

teNeues Publishing Company
7 West 18th Street
New York, NY 10011, USA
Phone: 001-212-627-9090
Fax: 001-212-627-9511

teNeues Publishing UK Ltd.
12 Ferndene Road
SE24 0AQ, UK
Phone: +44-(0)20-3542-8997
Fax: 0044-20-3542-8997

teNeues France S.A.R.L.
39, rue des Billets
18250 Henrichemont, France
Phone: 0033-2-4826-9348
Fax: 0033-1-7072-3482

While we strive for utmost precision in every detail, we cannot be
held responsible for any inaccuracies, neither for any subsequent
loss or damage arising.

Bibliographic information published by the Deutsche Nationalbibliothek.
The Deutsche Nationalbibliothek lists this publication in the
Deutsche Nationalbibliografie; detailed bibliographic data are available
in the Internet at http://dnb.d-nb.de.

ISBN: 978-3-8327-9742-3
Library of Congress Control Number: 2013940495

Printed in China

**teNeues Publishing Group**
Kempen
Berlin
Cologne
Düsseldorf
Hamburg
London
Munich
New York
Paris

**teNeues**

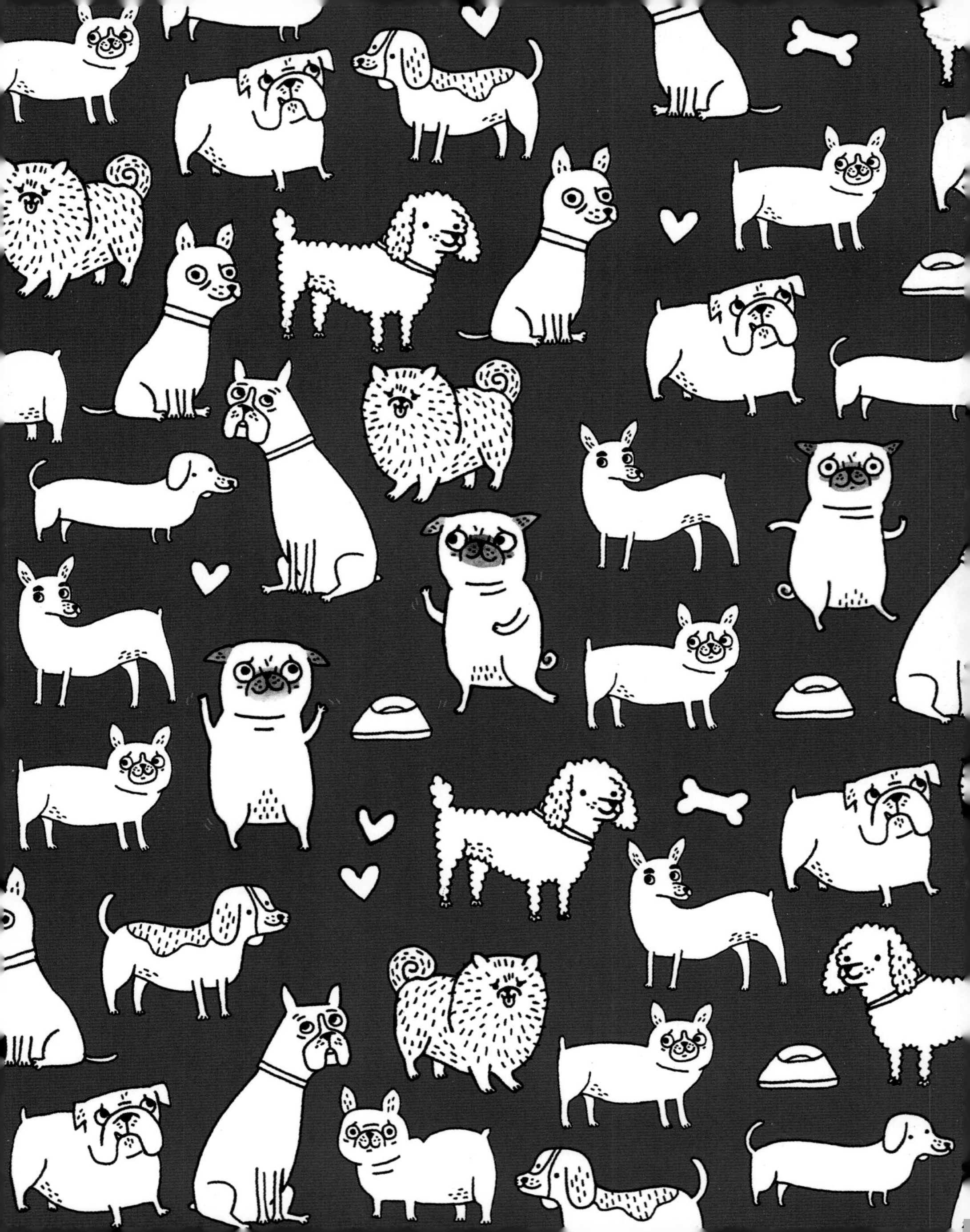